The Aquarian Su

TAU

Bernard Fitzwalter has been interested in astrology since he was about six, when he played King Herod's astrologer in his primary school nativity play. For the past six years he has been teaching astrology for the Marylebone-Paddington Institute, and for seven years he has had a regular column in OVER 21 magazine. In 1984 he appeared in the first series of Anglia Television's *Zodiac Game*, which prompted the *Daily Mirror* to say that he was 'enough to give astrology a good name'.

AQUARIAN SUN SIGN GUIDES

TAURUS

20 APRIL ~ 21 MAY

Bernard Fitzwalter

Cover illustration by Steinar Lund
Cover typography by Steven Lee

THE AQUARIAN PRESS
Wellingborough, Northamptonshire

First published 1987

British Library Cataloguing in Publication Data

Fitzwalter, Bernard
Taurus.—(The Aquarian sun sign guides)
1. Zodiac
I. Title
133.5'2   BF1726

ISBN 0-85030-575-6

The Aquarian Press is part of the
Thorsons Publishing Group

Printed and bound in Great Britain

Contents

PART 4: TAURUS TRIVIA

Introduction

This book has been written to help you find out a little about astrology and a lot about yourself. It explains, for the first time, the motives and aims that guide your actions and make you do things the way you do; what it does not do is give you a list of 'typical Taurus' things to see if you recognize any of them. You are not likely to be typical anything: you are unique. What you *do* have in common with others who have birthdays at about the same time as you is a way of using your energy, a way of thinking, a set of motives and beliefs which seem to make sense to you, and which other people, those of the other eleven signs, obviously do not have. This book shows you those motives and beliefs, and shows you how they fit in with those of the other eleven signs. The zodiac is like a jigsaw: all the pieces have to be there for the whole picture to emerge.

This book also sets out to answer some very simple questions which are often asked but seldom answered. Questions like 'Why does the zodiac have twelve signs?' and 'What does being a Taurus actually mean?' as well as 'Why are Taureans supposed to be placid? Why can't they be temperamental instead?' and 'Why don't all the people of the same star sign look the same?'

The reason that these questions are seldom answered is because all too many astrologers don't know the rudiments of astrological theory, and what they do know they don't tell, because they think it is too difficult for the man in the street to understand. This is obvious nonsense: astrology was devised for and by people who did not normally read or write as much as we do, nor did they all have PhDs or the equivalent. The man in the street is quite capable of understanding anything provided that it is shown simply and clearly, from first principles upwards, and provided he has sufficient interest. Buying this book is evidence enough of your interest, and I hope that the explanations are simple enough and clear enough for you. If they are not, it is my fault, and not that of astrology.

How to Use this Book

The book is in four parts. It is best to read them in sequence, but if you have neither time nor patience, then they each work individually. Part 2 does not assume that you have read Part 1, though it helps. Part 3 makes a lot more sense if you have already read Parts 1 and 2, but it isn't mandatory. Part 4, although just as firmly based on astrological principles as the other three, is deliberately intended as light relief.

The first part of the book deals with the theory behind the zodiac; it sets out the principles of astrology and enables you to see why Taurus is assigned the qualities it has, how the ruling planet system works, and what all the other signs are like in terms of motivation, so you can compare them to your own. There is a short and effective method given for assessing the aims and motives of other people. When you read Part 3 you will need to know a bit about the other signs, as you will be finding out that you have more to you than just the Taurus part you knew about.

The second part describes the essential Taurus. It shows you how there are different sorts of Taureans according to where your birthday falls in the month, and shows how Taurean energy is used differently in the Taurean as a child, adult, and parent.

Since you spend the greatest part of your life in dealing with other individuals, the way Taurus deals with relationships is treated in some detail. This is the largest section of the book.

The third part shows you a different kind of zodiac, and

enables you to go into your own life in much greater detail. It isn't complicated, but you do need to think. It crosses the border between the kind of astrology you get in the magazines, and the sort of thing a real astrologer does. There's no reason why you can't do it yourself because, after all, you know yourself best.

The fourth part shows you the surface of being a Taurean, and how that zodiacal energy comes out in your clothes, your home, even your favourite food. The final item of this part actually explains the mechanics of being lucky, which you probably thought was impossible.

I hope that when you finish reading you will have a clearer view of yourself, and maybe like yourself a little more. Don't put the book away and forget about it; read it again in a few months' time—you will be surprised at what new thoughts about yourself it prompts you to form!

Note

Throughout this book, the pronouns 'he', 'him', and 'his' have been used to describe both male and female. Everything which applies to a male Taurean applies to a female Taurean as well. There are two reasons why I have not bothered to make the distinction: firstly, to avoid long-windedness; secondly, because astrologically there is no need. It is not possible to tell from a horoscope whether the person to whom it relates is male or female, because to astrology they are both living individuals full of potential.

BERNARD FITZWALTER

Part 1

How the Zodiac Works

1. The Meaning of the Zodiac

Two Times Two is Four; Four Times Three is Twelve

It is no accident that there are twelve signs in the zodiac, although there are a great many people who reckon themselves to be well versed in astrology who do not know the reasons why, and cannot remember ever having given thought to the principles behind the circle of twelve.

The theory is quite simple, and once you are familiar with it, it will enable you to see the motivation behind all the other signs as well as your own. What's more, you only have to learn nine words to do it. That's quite some trick—being able to understand what anybody else you will ever meet is trying to do, with nine words.

It works like this.

The zodiac is divided into twelve signs, as you know. Each of the twelve represents a stage in the life cycle of solar energy as it is embodied in the life of mankind here on our planet. There are tides in this energy; sometimes it flows one way, sometimes another, like the tides of the ocean. Sometimes it is held static, in the form of an object, and sometimes it is released when that object is broken down after a period of time. The twelve signs show all these processes, both physical and spiritual, in their interwoven pattern.

Six signs are used to show the flowing tide, so to speak, and six for the ebbing tide. Aries, Gemini, Leo, Libra, Sagittarius, and Aquarius are the 'flowing' group, and the others form the second group. You will notice at once that the signs alternate, one with the other, around the zodiac, so that the movement is maintained, and there is never a concentration of one sort of energy in one place. People whose Sun sign is in the first group tend to radiate their energies outwards from themselves. They are the ones who like to make the first move, like to be the ones to take command of a situation, like to put something of themselves into whatever they are doing. They don't feel right standing on the sidelines; they are the original have-a-go types. Energy comes out of them and is radiated towards other people, in the same way as the Sun's energy is radiated out to the rest of the solar system.

The people in the other signs are the opposite to that, as you would expect. They collect all the energy from the first group, keeping it for themselves and making sure none is wasted. They absorb things from a situation or from a personal contact, rather than contributing to it. They prefer to watch and learn rather than make the first move. They correspond to the Moon, which collects and reflects the energy of the Sun. One group puts energy out, one group takes it back in. The sum total of energy in the universe remains constant, and the two halves of the zodiac gently move to and fro with the tide of the energies.

This energy applies both to the real and concrete world of objects, as well as to the intangible world of thoughts inside our heads.

A distinction has to be made, then, between the real world and the intangible world. If this is done, we have four kinds of energy: outgoing and collecting, physical and mental. These four kinds of energy have been recognized for a long time, and were given names to describe the way they work more than two thousand years ago. These are the elements. All the energy in the cosmos can be described in the terms of these four: Fire, Earth, Air, Water.

Fire is used to describe that outgoing energy which applies to the real and physical world. There are three signs given to it: Aries, Leo, and Sagittarius. People with the Sun in any of these

signs find themselves with the energy to get things going. They
are at their best when making a personal contribution to a
situation, and they expect to see some tangible results for their
efforts. They are sensitive to the emotional content of anything,
but that is not their prime concern, and so they tend to let it look
after itself while they busy themselves with the actual matter in
hand. Wherever you meet Fire energy in action, it will be shown
as an individual whose personal warmth and enthusiasm are
having a direct effect on his surroundings.

Earth is used to describe the real and physical world where the
energies are being collected and stored, sometimes in the form
of material or wealth. The three signs given to the element are
Taurus, Virgo, and Capricorn. Where Fire energy in people
makes them want to move things, Earth energy makes them want
to hold things and stop them moving. The idea of touching and
holding, and so that of possession, is important to these people,
and you can usually see it at work in the way they behave
towards their own possessions. The idea is to keep things stable,
and to hold energy stored for some future time when it will be
released. Earth Sun people work to ensure that wherever they are
is secure and unlikely to change; if possible they would like the
strength and wealth of their situation to increase, and will work
towards that goal. Wherever you meet Earth energy in action,
there will be more work being done than idle chat, and there will
be a resistance to any kind of new idea. There will be money
being made, and accumulated. The idea of putting down roots
and bearing fruit may be a useful one to keep in mind when
trying to understand the way this energy functions.

Air is used to describe outgoing mental energies; put more
simply, this is communication. Here the ideas are formed in the
mind of the individual, and put out in the hope that they can
influence and meet the ideas of another individual; this is
communication, in an abstract sense. Gemini, Libra, and
Aquarius are all Air signs, and people with the Sun in those signs
are very much concerned with communicating their energies to
others. Whether anything gets done as a result of all the
conversation is not actually important; if there is to be a

concrete result, then that is the province of Fire or Earth energies. Here the emphasis is on shaping the concept, not the reality. There is an affinity with Fire energies, because both of them are outgoing, but other than that they do not cross over into each other's territory. Wherever you meet Air energy in action, there is a lot of talk, and new ideas are thrown up constantly, but there is no real or tangible result, no real product, and no emotional involvement; were there to be emotional content, the energies would be watery ones.

Water is the collection of mental energies. It is the response to communication or action. It absorbs and dissolves everything else, and puts nothing out. In a word, it is simply feelings. Everything emotional is watery by element, because it is a response to an outside stimulus, and is often not communicated. It is not, at least not in its pure sense, active or initiatory, and it does not bring anything into being unless transformed into energy of a different type, such as Fire. Cancer, Scorpio and Pisces are the Water signs, and natives of those signs are often moody, withdrawn, and uncommunicative. Their energy collects the energy of others, and keeps their mental responses to external events stored. They are not being sad for any particular reason; it is simply the way that energy works. It is quite obvious that they are not showing an outgoing energy, but neither have they anything tangible to show for their efforts, like the money and property which seem to accumulate around Earth people. Water people simply absorb, keep to themselves, and do not communicate. To the onlooker, this appears unexciting, but there again the onlooker is biased: Fire and Air energies only appreciate outgoing energy forms, Earth energies recognize material rather than mental energies, and other Water energies are staying private and self-contained!

We now recognize four kinds of energy. Each of these comes in three distinct phases; if one zodiac sign is chosen to represent each of these phases within an element, there would be twelve different kinds of energy, and that would define the zodiac of twelve, with each one showing a distinct and different phase of the same endless flow of energy.

The first phase, not surprisingly, is a phase of definition, where the energies take that form for the first time, and where they are at their purest; they are not modified by time or circumstance, and what they aim to do is to start things in their own terms. These four most powerful signs (one for each element, remember) are called cardinal signs: Aries, Cancer, Libra, Capricorn. When the Sun enters any of these signs, the seasons change; the first day of the Sun's journey through Aries is the first day of spring, and the Spring equinox; Libra marks the Autumnal equinox, while Cancer and Capricorn mark Midsummer's Day and the shortest day respectively.

The second phase is where the energy is mature, and spreads itself a little; it is secure in its place, and the situation is well established, so there is a sort of thickening and settling of the energy flow. Here it is at its most immobile, even Air. The idea is one of maintenance and sustenance, keeping things going and keeping them strong. This stage is represented by Taurus, Leo, Scorpio, and Aquarius, and they are called, unsurprisingly, fixed signs. These four signs, and their symbols, are often taken to represent the four winds and the four directions North, South, East and West. Their symbols (with an eagle instead of a scorpion for Scorpio) turn up all over Europe as tokens for the evangelists Luke, Mark, John and Matthew (in that order).

The final phase is one of dissolution and change, as the energy finds itself applied to various purposes, and in doing so is changed into other forms. There is an emphasis on being used for the good, but being used up nonetheless. The final four signs are Gemini, Virgo, Sagittarius, and Pisces; in each of them the energies of their element are given back out for general use and benefit from where they had been maintained in the fixed phase. It is this idea of being used and changed which leads to this phase being called mutable.

Three phases of energy, then; one to form, one to grow strong and mature, and one to be used, and to become, at the end, something else. Like the waxing, full, and waning phases of the Moon.

The diagram on page 16 shows the twelve signs arranged in

their sequence round the zodiac. Notice how cleverly the cycle and phases interweave:

(a) Outgoing and collecting energies alternate, with no two the same next to each other;

(b) Physical ebb and flow are followed by mental ebb and flow alternately in pairs round the circle, meaning that the elements follow in sequence round the circle three times;

(c) Cardinal, fixed, and mutable qualities follow in sequence round the circle four times, and yet

(d) No two elements or qualities the same are next to each other, even though their sequences are not broken.

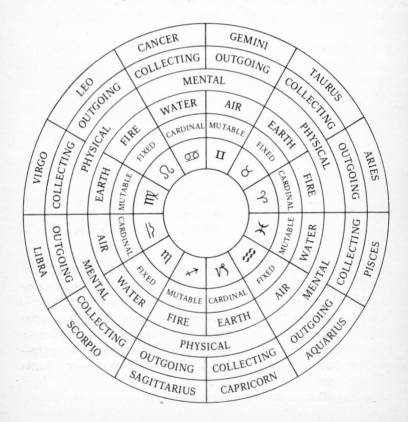

The interweaving is perfect. The zodiac shows all forms of energy, physical and mental, outgoing or incoming, waxing or waning, harmoniously forming a perfectly balanced unity when all the components are taken together. Humanity, as a whole, contains all the possibilities; each individual is a component necessary to the whole.

All this can be a bit long-winded when what you want is some way of holding all that information for instant recall and use, which is where the nine words come in.

If a single word is used for the kind of energy flow, and another two for the element and quality, then they can be used to form a sentence which will describe the way the energy is being used.

As a suggestion (use other words if they are more meaningful to you), try 'outgoing' and 'collecting' for the energy flows.

Next, for the elements:

Fire :	activity	(Aries, Leo, Sagittarius)
Earth:	material	(Taurus, Virgo, Capricorn)
Air :	communication	(Gemini, Libra, Aquarius)
Water:	feelings	(Cancer, Scorpio, Pisces)

And for the qualities:

Cardinal :	defining	(Aries, Cancer, Libra, Capricorn)
Fixed :	maintaining	(Taurus, Leo, Scorpio, Aquarius)
Mutable :	using	(Gemini, Virgo, Sagittarius, Pisces)

Now in answer to the question 'What is a Gemini doing?' and answer can be formed as 'He's outgoing, and he's using communication', which neatly encapsulates the motivation of the sign. All that you need to know about the guiding principles of a Gemini individual, no matter who he is, is in that sentence. He will never deviate from that purpose, and you can adapt your own actions to partner or oppose his intention as you please.

A Scorpio? He's collecting, and he's maintaining his feelings. An Arian? He's outgoing, and he's defining activity. And so on.

Those nine words, or some similar ones which you like better, can be used to form effective and useful phrases which describe the motivation of everybody you will ever meet. How different people show it is their business, but their motivation and purpose is clear if you know their birthday.

Remember, too, that this motivation works at all levels, from the immediate to the eternal. The way a Taurean conducts himself in today's problems is a miniature of the way he is trying to achieve his medium-term ambitions over the next two or three years. It is also a miniature of his whole existence: when, as an old man, he looks back to see what he tried to do and what he achieved, both the efforts and the achievement, whatever it is, can be described in the same phrase with the same three words.

2. The Planets and the Horseshoe

You will have heard, or read, about the planets in an astrological context. You may have a horoscope in a magazine which says that Mars is here or Jupiter is there, and that as a consequence this or that is likely to happen to you. Two questions immediately spring to mind: What do the planets signify? How does that affect an individual?

The theory is straightforward again, and not as complex as that of the zodiac signs in the previous chapter. Remember that the basic theory of astrology is that since the universe and mankind are part of the same Creation, they both move in a similar fashion, so Man's movements mirror those of the heavens. So far, so good. If you look at the sky, night after night, or indeed day after day, it looks pretty much the same; the stars don't move much in relationship to each other, at least not enough to notice. What do move, though, are the Sun and Moon, and five other points of light—the planets. It must therefore follow that if these are the things which move, they must be the things which can be related to the movements of Man. Perhaps, the theory goes, they have areas of the sky in which they feel more at home, where the energy that they represent is stronger; there might be other places where they are uncomfortable and weak, corresponding to the times in your life when you just can't win no matter what you do. The planets would then behave like ludo counters, moving round the heavens trying to get back to a home of their own colour, and then starting a new game.

The scheme sounds plausible, makes a sort of common sense, and is endearingly human; all hallmarks of astrological thought, which unlike scientific thought has to relate everything to the human experience. And so it is: the planets are given values to show the universal energy in different forms, and given signs of the zodiac as homes. Therefore your Sun sign also has a planet to look after it, and the nature of that planet will show itself strongly in your character.

The planets used are the Sun and Moon, which aren't really planets at all, one being a satellite and the other a star, and then Mercury, Venus, Mars, Jupiter, and Saturn. This was enough until the eighteenth century, when Uranus was discovered, followed in the subsequent two hundred years by Neptune and Pluto. Some modern astrologers put the three new planets into horoscopes, but it really isn't necessary, and may not be such a good idea anyway. There are three good reasons for this:

(a)   The modern planets break up the symmetry of the original system, which was perfectly harmonious;

(b)   The old system is still good enough to describe everything that can happen in a human life, and the modern planets have little to add;

(c)   Astrology is about the relationship between the sky and a human being. An ordinary human being cannot see the outer planets on his own; he needs a telescope. We should leave out of the system such things as are of an extra-human scale or magnitude: they do not apply to an ordinary human. If we put in things which are beyond ordinary human capabilities, we cannot relate them to the human experience, and we are wasting our time.

In the diagram on page 21 the zodiac is presented in its usual form, but it has also been split into two from the start of Leo to the start of Aquarius. The right hand half is called the solar half, and the other one is the lunar half. The Sun is assigned to Leo because in the Northern hemisphere, where astrology started, August is when you feel the influence of the Sun most, especially in the Eastern Mediterranean, where the Greeks and the other early Western civilizations were busy putting the framework of astrology together in the second millennium BC. The Sun is important because it gives light. The Moon gives light too; it is reflected sunlight, but it is enough to see by, and this is enough to give the Sun and Moon the title of 'the Lights' in astrology. The Moon is assigned to Cancer, so that the two of them can balance and complement each other. From there, moving away from the Lights around the circle on both sides, the signs have the planets assigned to them starting with the fastest mover, Mercury, and continuing in decreasing order of speed. Saturn is the slowest mover of all, and the two signs opposite to

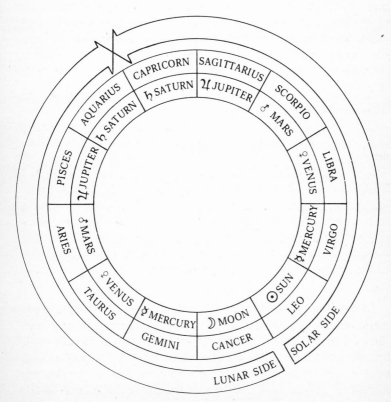

the Lights are both governed by that planet. The reasons for this apparent assymmetry will be explained in a little while. This arrangement is, of course, the horseshoe of the title to this chapter.

The Sun and Moon work in a similar fashion to the outgoing and collecting energies we noted earlier with the twelve signs. The Sun is radiant above all else; energy comes outwards from it, warming and energizing all those around it. Leo people, whose sign is the Sun's, work like this by being at the centre of a group of people and acting as inspiration and encouragement to them all. The Moon reflects the Sun's light, and energies of a lunar kind are directed inwards towards the core of the person. The two energies are necessarily linked; lunar people would starve without the solar folks' warmth, but the solar types need someone to radiate to or their purpose is unfulfilled.

The planets on each side of the horseshoe display their own energies in a solar or lunar way depending on which side of the pattern they are on.

Mercury and Venus form a pair, representing complementary but opposite ideas, which should be familiar by now. Mercury represents difference, and Venus stands for similarity.

Wherever anything new forms that is distinguishable from the background, then Mercury is there making it what it is, highlighting what makes it different. Anything separate is Mercurial, and words, since they are separate and can be strung together into millions of different combinations, are Mercurial too. Mercury is not a long-term influence; it notes things as being different for an instant, and then they become part of the establishment, and something else is new elsewhere. Because 'new' is an instantaneous state—that is, something can only be new once, and for a moment—Mercury is not associated with anything lasting, and its rapid motion as a planet leads to its being associated with the idea of speed. Virgo, Mercury's solar sign, is concerned with the changing of the shape of things ('collecting, using material' in our keyword system), while Gemini, the lunar sign, is concerned with reading and writing, and getting new ideas ('outgoing, using communication').

Venus does the reverse; it looks for that which is similar, finding points of contact to make relationships between common interests and energies. It likes to preserve the harmonies of life, and resents anything which might interrupt them. Love and affection are naturally Venusian, but so is music and all of the Arts, for the harmonies they contain. Expressed in a solar way, Venus is Libra, the maker of relationships; its lunar face is Taurus, emphasizing food and furnishings as things which give pleasure to the individual.

The next pair are Mars and Jupiter. Mars applies force from the outside to impose structure on a disordered universe, while Jupiter expands forcibly from the inside to give growth and wealth, inviting everyone else to join in.

Mars is pure force, energy in a straight line with a direction to go in. Anger and passion are both Martian, and so is lust, because they are all examples of great energy directed towards a given end. Note that Martian force is not necessarily strength, wealth, or know-how, just pure energy, which often boils over and needs controlling. Mars is the power in an athlete, and in an assassin too. It is also the power in a lover, because the urge to create is also the urge to pro-create, and if that energy fulfils its purpose then that creation takes place. Scorpio is its solar side, the power to control and create; in lunar form it is shown by Aries, as energy enjoyed for its own sake by its owner, with no purpose except to express it.

Jupiter is the spirit of expansion from within; not only does it oppose Mars' force from outside, it opposes Mars' physicality with its own mental emphasis. Jupiter develops the mind, then. As it does so, it develops all natural talents of an academic nature, and encourages movement, enquiry and travel to broaden experience and knowledge. The Solar expression of this is Sagittarius, where the centaur symbol is both a wise teacher and a free-roaming wild horse at the same time. Jupiter in a lunar sense is Pisces, where the imagination is developed to a greater extent than anywhere else, but used to provide an internal dream world for the owner's pleasure. Great sensitivity here, but the lunar energies are not of the sort to be expressed; rather other energies are *im*pressed on the Piscean mind.

Saturn is the last of the five planets. He stands alone, and if it is necessary to consider him as paired with anything it is with the Lights as an entity together. The Lights are at the centre of the system; Saturn is at its edge. They are the originators of the energies of the zodiac, and he is the terminator. Everything to do with limits and ends is his. He represents Time, and lots of it, in contrast to Mercury, which represented the instant. He represents the sum total of all things, and the great structures and frameworks of long-term endeavour. In solar form he is Capricorn, the representative of hard work, all hierarchies, and all rulers; in lunar form he is Aquarius, showing the horizontal structure of groups of people within society at different levels. Here he denies the activity of Mars, because society is too big for one person to change against the collective will, and he contains the expansion of Jupiter within himself. Venus and Mercury can neither relate to it nor make it change, because it is always the same, in the end.

The planets show important principles in action, the same as the zodiac does. You have probably noticed that the horseshoe of the planets and the ring of the zodiac say the same thing in a different way, and that is true about most things in astrology. It may be that the two systems interrelate and overlap because they are from the same source: after all, $3+2+2=7$, which is the planet's total, and $3x2x2=12$, which is the signs'. How you assign the elements and qualities, pairs of planets and lights is for you to decide. The joy of astrology, like all magic, is that it has you at the centre, and is made to fit its user's requirements. Now you know the principles, you can use it as you please, and as it seems relevant to you.

Part 2
Yourself—and Others

3. The Essential Taurus

All the energy in the zodiac is solar, but that solar energy takes many forms. It is moderated and distributed through the planetary energies until it finally shows in you, the individual. As a Taurus, the prime planetary energy is that of Venus; you will be motivated by, and behave in the manner of, the energies of Venus. To remind yourself of what that means, read the section on Venus on page 23. As a sign of the zodiac, Taurus is a Fixed Earth sign. Remind yourself what that means by reading page 13 Now we have to see how those essential principles work when expressed through a person and his motivation.

What it Means to be a Taurus

You know what it is to be a Taurus, because you are one; but you probably don't know what it is that makes a Taurus the way he is, because you cannot stand outside yourself. You would have to be each of the other eleven signs in turn to understand the nature of the energy that motivates you. This essential energy is in every Taurean, but it shows itself to different extents and in different ways. Because it is in every single Taurean, it is universal rather than specific, and universal ideas tend to come in language which sounds a little on the woolly side. You will think that it isn't really about what makes you who you are, because you don't feel like that every day—or at least you think you don't. In fact, you feel like that all the time, but you don't notice it any more than you notice your eyes focusing, yet they do it all the time, and you see things the way you do because of it.

The first thing to note is that the zodiac is a circle, not a line with a beginning and an end. If it were a line, then Taurus would be near the start of it, but that would be to miss the point; if the zodiac is a circle, then Taurus is a stage in an endlessly repeating cycle, and we will get a much better idea of what it is if we look to see where it came from, and where it is going.

The sign before Taurus is Aries. Aries represents the start of all that is new; it is the initial surge of energy that defines and gives life to any new organism. Everything has to start somewhere, and as it starts—is shaped, forged, or born—it is partaking of the Arian phase of its existence. Aries gives no thought to how anything should continue or maintain itself, not even to how it should grow; initiation is all. Once started, however, the organism needs to sustain itself, protect itself, and feed itself. In short, it needs to ensure that its own requirements are met, and to provide a safe environment for its continued existence.

This self-protecting, self-nourishing, growing phase is what Taurus is all about. Taurean energies are those directed towards providing security and nourishment for the self. Only when this phase is fully completed, and all is secure, can the organism start to take an interest in the world outside, and consider communicating with other organisms—and that communicative phase is Gemini.

From this sequence of signs you can see how the Taurean has his place in the cycle, and you will no doubt recognize a few of the deeper facets of the Taurean character in the sequence too. Taureans would rather do anything than give up and start again. Starting things is the last thing they want to do, and the last thing they will ever consider as a course of action. It is because the idea of starting is Aries, and it is behind them in the cycle; they feel that starting over again would be a backward step. As a last resort they will consider it. Every sign considers the activities of the sign behind it as the emergencies-only, against-their-better-judgement course of action. Conversely, Taureans aren't usually very good at putting their thoughts into words, and would dearly love to have the verbal dexterity of the Gemini. To all signs, the qualities of the next sign on in the cycle seem irresistibly glamorous. It's not that Taureans don't think much; it's rather that they don't talk much. Sometimes they don't know what they think, but they know what they feel, which is an organic process, done with the whole body, rather than just inside the head.

The Taurean measures himself by what he can touch or feel. His instrument of discernment is not his mind, but his five senses—in particular taste and touch. When you are surrounded by things which you know are yours and are likely to remain so, then you are comfortable. A Taurean likes to know where his next meal is coming from, and where he is likely to rest his head this evening—in fact, they are his main concerns. An ever-changing world where things are never the same twice, and where the most recent things become rapidly out of date, is upsetting for the Taurean mind.

Let us look at the Taurean approach to the world from three key points of view. Taken together, they will show you the whole of what a Taurean tries to do with his world. These points of view are stability, possession, and nourishment.

Stability is absolutely essential for your happiness, Taurus. As the first earth sign of the zodiac, your roots and where you live are of prime importance to you. You can reassure yourself about the rightness of your existence if you know where you are; familiar surroundings enable you to orientate yourself properly. If you are in strange surroundings, or for some reason your usual routines are disrupted, then you start to worry, and the old uncertainties about where your next meal is coming from start to surface. You define yourself in relation to your surroundings, so if the surroundings are unfamiliar to you, then you don't know who you are. It's as simple as that.

You are obviously going to try to maintain stability in your life and circumstances, if only to maintain some sort of consistency in your view of yourself. Don't forget that you are a fixed sign, and they are the ones which like to keep things, as far as possible, just the way they are, even if they are not particularly favourable; change is always seen as something to be avoided (yet at the same time rather dangerous and exciting, because it is a quality of the next sign on, as we noticed earlier). This desire to be rooted in the earth, to be in the same place for ever, like a tree, can lead to some problems in itself. You could get blown over by a wind, killed by a drought, or cut down by a woodcutter; in other words, you cannot adapt to changing circumstances, nor do you move when it would be in your interest to do so. Other people see this insistence on stability as sheer stubbornness, though on good days they will be quick to label you as constant and dependable, too.

Possession follows on from the desire for stability. The best way to make unfamiliar things familiar is to own them; over a period of time you can get used to them, and feel secure in their possession. If they are yours, they are not likely to be taken away again or wander off, and this adds to their stable status in your mind. Consequently, a Taurean likes to acquire things, and enjoys the things he owns. Since you see yourself in the things you own, and since you define yourself by your surroundings, you are likely to have a very comfortable and well-furnished home, and enjoy being in it. Other zodiac types use their homes to live in or to work in, but only you use it as an extension of yourself. You are like your home, and it is like you; friends and guests will be able to see your character very clearly from the decoration and furnishings, which they cannot so easily do in a non-Taurean house. Of course, you are equally keen to possess and make stable all the intangibles in your life, too; this means that you are very possessive of your loved ones, and will be deeply wounded by any separation. If someone in whom you have placed a lot of trust and affection goes out of your life, you feel insecure, because things have become unstable again, and your emotional stability and nourishment have been interrupted. As you no doubt know, this can grow into jealousy and a suffocating possessiveness; on the other hand, your loyalty, devotion, and unwavering constancy are the envy of anyone who wishes that love was, for them at least, for keeps. It certainly is for you.

Nourishment is essential to the Taurean. Where the Arian uses his body as a vehicle for his energy, the Taurean uses his body to live in; it has to be kept going, and all its requirements met. Food is more than just something to eat; for you, it is a reminder that you have a physical existence, and that you are maintaining it. This in turn is reassuring, and so the feeling of stability and security is reinforced. You eat well, and you like eating; not surprisingly, you take great interest in food, and make it reflect your opinion of yourself, as you do with everything you own. After all, if you ate rubbish, it would show what a low opinion of yourself you had, wouldn't it? To reassure and remind yourself, you make sure that what you eat is to your taste, and of high quality. Emotional nourishment is attended to in the same way, as are bodily comforts. Taureans like to be liked; it provides emotional nourishment, and a form of reassurance.

You can see how stability, possession, and nourishment all work together to the same end—security. Whatever a Taurus does is towards this ultimate end.

Physically, the sign corresponds to the throat and neck. This seems a little odd until you think about it. The neck supports the head, which is the important bit of your body; the idea of support is very Taurean. The throat contains the tubes through which you take in food, water, and air; nourishment of every kind, in fact. There you will find also some of the glands whose work is to stabilize and maintain the whole of the body as it grows. All very Taurean. Glandular diseases are, not surprisingly, common to Taureans who have to deal with too much instability at once. There are other considerations to take into account when discussing diseases, though, and some of them are examined in 'The Year within Each Day' (p. 67).

Taureans often have thick necks, but they also have lovely voices, because that's where their larynx is. Many of them sing well, and most of them are musical, because music is soothing to listen to; a familiar aural environment, this time!

To sum up, if you want a single picture which encapsulates the spirit of Taurus, look no further than the zodiac picture of the bull. Fierce when roused, very territorial, but quite content to live in his field and munch the grass unless disturbed. Leave him alone and he's very happy with things as they are.

Early, Middle or Late? The Decanates

Each of the zodiac signs is divided into degrees, like an arc of any other circle. Since a circle has 360 degrees, then each sign must be 30 degrees, since there are twelve signs. Each of the signs is further split into sections of ten degrees, called decanates. There are three decanates in each sign, and the one that your birthday falls in will tell you a little more about how that Taurean energy actually works in you as an individual.

First decanate (20–29 April)
This is the purest form of Taurus, where there is a double helping of Venus's energies, seeking everything that is amenable and pleasant. Early Taureans are the most comfort-loving of the sign, and the ones with the greatest liking for anything soft. Soft clothes in soft fabrics which have a pleasant feel to them are appealing to you; it is the direct, tangible reassurance of a comforting substance which Venus would like you to appreciate. You are also the most artistic and discerning in your tastes, compared to the other two decanates. Taureans have a very good sense of colour and design, and the influence of Venus is going to make sure that you never have two clashing colours close together. Venus will also make you the Taurean who is the most appreciative of his food; you will spend much time in its preparation.

   Emotionally, you are likely to need a lot of reassurance, and will be overly fond of anyone who offers you comfort and companionship. You don't like arguing with people, even if you know that you are right, and will not be swayed from your point of view; the emotional disturbance generated by an argument of any kind is something which you just can't bear.

Second decanate (30 April–10 May)
This time Venus gets a little help from Mercury, and the intense

feeling of softness and vulnerability is moderated to some extent. Mercury will help the mind and wit of this Taurean, so that these middle-of-the-sign bulls are the clearest-thinking of the sign, as well as being the ones with the best-developed sense of humour. Taureans aren't very verbal people at the best of times, but here those faculties are given a helping hand. The voice of the Taurean is at its best here, too.

Taurus is an earth sign, of course, and any material whatsoever is earthy by element. In this section of the sign, skills in working with any material come to the fore; Taureans who work with wood or metal, or those who like to use their Venusian sensibilities and work with food or furnishings, have an extra talent and facility given by Mercury in the central decanate of the sign.

Money is important to Taureans, too: it is something to acquire in itself, it can be used to acquire other things, and its possession gives security. Skill in the handling and acquisition of money also comes from Mercury to this decanate.

Third decanate (11—21 May)
The first decanate was receptive and comforting—the 'nourishment' mentioned earlier. The second decante is to do with acquisition and possession, and the use to which material is put. The last one is to do with possession and stability, and the maintenance of things in their positions. It is Taurus at its most solid and powerful; people with the Sun here don't need the comfort and reassurance that the earlier ones do, but they will do everything they can to hang on to whatever it is that they have. These are the Taureans who suffer long and hard rather than give up or change direction; these are the ones it is dangerous to goad into eventual action, because they are strong and angry defenders of what they see as their own. They take life seriously, with a strongly developed sense of duty. They get on with what they have to do without complaint, and when offered something different by way of diversion or entertainment, they will make sure that they have finished all their work first, and that all is secure and taken care of before they let themselves

relax a little. Perhaps it is because they are at the end of the sign that they feel they have so much to do before the next sign comes along!

Three Phases of Life: Taurus as Child, Adult, Parent

The Taurean child

The Taurean child is the one who gave rise to that overworked description of the moderate achiever at school—'he is a plodder'. It is true that Taurean children do plod, but they are thorough, and what they have learned, they remember for ever. They cannot be rushed; they assimilate things at their own pace, and do not move on to a new subject until the old one is thoroughly familiar and well known. Until the Taurean child feels that a certain technique or piece of knowledge has been examined from all angles, is familiar, and is unlikely to offer him any surprises when he returns to it, he will not move on. This rate of progress makes him a little slower than the rest of his class, but his sense of duty keeps him working in an attempt to keep up—hence the title of plodder, since he will always appear to be working very hard, yet will never make the rapid progress that other children do from time to time when a subject really interests them.

Taurean children are apt to be heavily built, and this can lead to some teasing at school. Unfortunately, since they represent by their very youthfulness the beginning of the sign (see first decanate, above, for the qualities peculiar to this end of the sign), they will compensate for their emotional discomfort by overeating, which can lead to health problems. Their heavy physique means that they seldom excel at individual sports, but their sense of duty, solidity, and support can make them useful members of sporting teams—they make very good second-row forwards in rugby!

Any artistic talents must be encouraged. All Taureans have them, and they must be noticed and nurtured when they show in the child.

These children are possessive, like their parents. They are

unwilling to share their toys, books, or money with their friends, and they can get very jealous and resentful of affection transferred from them to a sibling or friend. They should be encouraged to be more open and generous—you won't change their essential nature, but you may stop them becoming obsessive at an early age!

The Taurean adult
The Taurean adult is solid and reliable, but never innovative or a motivator of others. He is careful to weigh things up before he makes a decision, and when the decision is made, he knows that it is based on all the available information. All this seems most laudable, but outsiders should note two things: firstly, the course of action decided upon will be the one which introduces the fewest new elements or procedures into the Taurean's established routine, and which involves him in no loss of position or possession at all; and secondly, the course of action decided upon is not modifiable in any way at all, even if new circumstances merit a serious rethink. The Taurean will admit neither of these things, but they need to be taken into account.

A resistance to change, and an unwillingness to modify their point of view, can mean that they are rapidly overtaken by events, and are not really at home in situations where they have to think quickly to react to a constantly changing challenge. They will make their own territory wherever they are, and do their job in it in their own way, oblivious of any new developments outside. The routine that they generate for themselves is itself a form of security for them. Anything which requires a steady effort over a long period is ideal for the Taurean; he possesses a stamina and an ability to apply himself over the long period which no other sign can match, and easily outlasts the Fire and Air signs.

Although not mean or miserly, Taureans do not throw money away. They spend it freely, but it is to their own benefit rather than anybody else's. When they keep money, it is for their own security rather than so that the world can see how rich they must be. Taureans enjoy their wealth directly and for themselves, which is what sets them apart from Capricorns in this respect.

The Taurean parent
A Taurean parent is very protective. He tries always to provide a
stable and comfortable environment for his child, where every
one of the child's needs are met. Since the adult knows how
important it is to him to have the security of his home and
surroundings, he feels that the child must surely have these
needs too and it is his duty to provide them. He also wants the
child to appreciate all that his parent has done for him, a process
which he sees as emotional reassurance for both of them. If the
child rebels at all, or spurns the parent's generosity, then it is the
parent who is upset, because there is an immediate instability as
the child leaves, coupled with a loss of possession as the child
takes with him all the time and emotional energy the parent
invested in him. These displays of independence are usual in
any home, but they are devastating to the Taurean parent, who
needs to tell himself that this is only to be expected, and a
natural process.

Taurean parents spoil their children with material comforts,
and feed them handsomely: 'mother's apple pie' is really
something if your mother is Taurean. As they get older, Taurean
parents become more and more accustomed to their home
routines, so the noise and disruption generated by teenage
children is very wearing on them: they find children as infants
much more rewarding. Letting go of their children when they
have had them for so long, so to speak, is the hardest thing
Taurean parents ever do.

4. Taurus Relationships

How Zodiacal Relationships Work

You might think that relationships between two people, described in terms of their zodiac signs, might come in 144 varieties; that is, twelve possible partners for each of the twelve signs. The whole business is a lot simpler than that. There are only seven varieties of relationship, although each of those has two people in it, of course, and the role you play depends on which end of the relationship you are at.

You may well have read before about how you are supposed to be suited to one particular sign or another. The truth is usually different. Taureans are supposed to get on with Virgos and Capricorns, and indeed they do, for the most part, but it is no use reading that if you have always found yourself attracted to Sagittarians, is it? There has to be a reason why you keep finding Sagittarians attractive, and it is not always to do with your Sun sign; other factors in your horoscope will have a lot to do with it. The reason you prefer people of certain signs as friends or partners is because the relationship of your sign to theirs produces the sort of qualities you are looking for, the sort of behaviour you find satisfactory. When you have identified which of the seven types of basic relationship it is, you can see which signs will produce that along with your own, and then read the motivation behind it explained later on in more detail in

'The Taurus Approach to Relationships' and the individual compatibility sections.

Look at the diagram on page 16. All you have to do is see how far away from you round the zodiacal circle your partner's Sun sign is. If they are Libra, they are five signs in front of you. You are also, of course, five signs behind them, which is also important, as you will see in a little while. If they are Aquarius, they are three signs behind you, and you are three signs in front of them. There are seven possibilities: you can be anything up to six signs apart, or you can both be of the same sign.

Here are the patterns of behaviour for the seven relationship types.

Same sign
Somebody who is of the same sign as you acts in the same way that you do, and is trying to achieve the same result for himself. If your goals permit two winners, this is fine, but if only one of you can be on top, you will argue. No matter how temperamental, stubborn, devious, or critical you can be, they can be just the same, and it may not be possible for you to take the same kind of punishment you hand out to others. In addition, they will display every quality which really annoys you about yourself, so that you are constantly reminded of it in yourself as well as in them. Essentially, you are fighting for the same space, and the amount of tolerance you have is the determining factor in the survival of this relationship.

One sign apart
Someone one sign forward from you acts as an environment for you to grow in. In time, you will take on those qualities yourself. When you have new ideas, they can often provide the encourage-ment to put them into practice, and seem to have all your requirements easily available. Often, it is this feeling that they already know all the pitfalls that you are struggling over which can be annoying; they always seem to be one step ahead of you, and can seemingly do without effort all the things which you have to sweat to achieve. If the relationship works well, they are

helpful to you, but there can be bitterness and jealousy if it doesn't.

Someone one sign back from you can act as a retreat from the pressures of the world. They seem to understand your particular needs for rest and recovery, whatever they may be, and can usually provide them. They can hold and understand your innermost secrets and fears; indeed, their mind works best with the things you fear most, and the fact that they can handle these so easily is a great help to you. If the relationship is going through a bad patch, their role as controller of your fears gets worrying, and you will feel unnerved in their presence, as though they were in control of you. When things are good, you feel secure with them behind you.

Two signs apart
Someone two signs forward from you acts like a brother or sister. They are great friends, and you feel equals in each other's company; there is no hint of the parent-child or master-servant relationship. They encourage you to talk, even if you are reticent in most other company; the most frequently heard description of these relationships is 'We make each other laugh'. Such a partner can always help you put into words the things that you want to say, and is there to help you say them. This is the relationship that teenagers enjoy with their 'best friend'. There is love, but it does not usually take sexual form, because both partners know that it would spoil the relationship by adding an element of unnecessary depth and weight.

Someone two signs behind you is a good friend and companion, but not as intimate as somebody two signs forward. They are the sort of people you love to meet socially; they are reliable and honest, but not so close that things become suffocatingly intense. They stop you getting too serious about life, and turn your thoughts outwards instead of inwards, involving you with other people. They stop you from being too selfish, and help you give the best of yourself to others. This relationship, then, has a cool end and a warm end; the leading sign feels much closer to his partner than the trailing sign does, but they are both satisfied by the relationship. They particularly value its chatty quality, the fact that it works even better when in a group, and its tone of affection and endearment rather than passion and obsession.

Three signs apart
Someone three signs in front of you represents a challenge of some kind or another. The energies of the pair of you can never run parallel, and so must meet at some time or another. Not head on, but across each other, and out of this you can both make something strong and well established which will serve the two of you as a firm base for the future. You will be surprised to find how fiercely this person will fight on your behalf, or for your protection; you may not think you need it, and you will be surprised that anybody would think of doing it, but it is so nonetheless.

Someone three signs behind you is also a challenge, and for the same reasons as stated above; from this end of the relationship, though, they will help you achieve the very best you are capable of in a material sense. They will see to it that you receive all the credit that is due to you for your efforts, and that everyone thinks well of you. Your reputation is their business, and they will do things with it that you could never manage yourself. It's like having your own P.R. team. This relationship works hard, gets results, and makes sure the world knows it. It also looks after itself, but it needs a lot of effort putting in.

Four signs apart
Someone four signs forward from you is the expression of yourself. All the things you wanted to be, however daring, witty, sexy, or whatever, they already are, and you can watch them doing it. They can also help you to be these things. They do things which you think are risky, and seem to get away with them. There are things you aim towards, sometimes a way of life that you would like to have, which these people seem to be able to live all the time; it doesn't seem to worry them that things might go wrong. There are lots of things in their life which frighten you, which you would lie awake at nights worrying

about, which they accept with a child's trust, and which never go wrong for them. You wish you could be like that.

Someone four signs behind you is an inspiration to you. All the things you wish you knew, they know already. They seem so wise and experienced, and you feel such an amateur; luckily, they are kind and caring teachers. They are convincing, too. When they speak, you listen and believe. It's nice to know there's somebody there with all the answers. This extraordinary relationship often functions as a mutual admiration society, with each end wishing it could be more like the other; unfortunately, it is far less productive than the three-sign separation, and much of its promise remains unfulfilled. Laziness is one of the inherent qualities of a four-sign separation; all its energies are fulfilled, and it rarely looks outside itself for something to act upon. Perhaps this is just as well for the rest of us.

Five signs apart
Someone five signs ahead of you is your technique. You know what you want to do; this person knows how to do it. He can find ways and means for you to do what you want to be involved in, and he can watch you while you learn and correct your mistakes. They know the right way to go about things, and have the clarity of thought and analytical approach necessary if you are to get things clear in your mind before you get started

Someone five signs behind you is your resource. Whenever you run out of impetus or energy, they step forward and support you. When you're broke, they lend you money, and seldom want it returned. When you need a steadying hand because you think you've over-reached yourself, they provide it. All this they do because they know that it's in their best interest as well as yours, to help you do things, and to provide the material for you to work with. You can always rely on them for help, and it's nice to know they will always be there. They cannot use all their talent on their own; they need you to show them how it should be done. Between you, you will use all that you both have to offer effectively and fully, but it is a relationship of cooperation and giving; not all the zodiac signs can make it work well enough.

Six signs apart

Someone six signs apart from you, either forwards or backwards, is both opponent and partner at the same time. You are both essentially concerned with the same area of life, and have the same priorities. Yet you both approach your common interests from opposite directions, and hope to use them in opposite ways. Where one is private, the other is public, and where one is self-centred, the other shares himself cheerfully. The failings in your own make-up are complemented by the strengths in the other; it is as if, between you, you make one whole person with a complete set of talents and capabilities. The problem with this partnership is that your complementary talents focus the pair of you on a single area of life, and this makes for not only a narrow outlook, but also a lack of flexibility in your response to changes. If the two of you are seeing everything in terms of career, or property, or personal freedom, or whatever, then you will have no way to deal effectively with a situation which cannot be dealt with in those terms. Life becomes like a seesaw; it alternates which end it has up or down, and can sometimes stay in balance; but it cannot swing round to face another way, and it is fixed to the ground so that it does not move.

These are the only combinations available, and all partnerships between two people can be described as a version of one of the seven types. It must be remembered, though, that some of the roles engendered by these dispositions of sign to sign are almost impossible to fulfil for some of the signs, because their essential energies, and the directions they are forced to take by the planets behind them, drive them in ways which make it too difficult. To form a relationship based on sharing and acceptance is one thing: to do it when you are governed by a planet like Mars is somethings else. Even when the relationship can form, the sort of approach produced by, say, Jupiter, is a very different thing from that produced by Venus.

The next thing you must consider, then, is how you, as a Taurean, attempt relationships as a whole, and what you try to find in them. Then you must lay the qualities and outlook of each of the twelve signs over the roles they must play in the seven relationship types, and see whether the pair of you manage to make the best of that relationship, or not.

The seven relationship types are common to all the signs, relating to all the other signs. You can use your understanding of them to analyse and understand the relationship between any pair of people that you know, whether or not they are Taurean; but to see how the characters fit into the framework in more detail, you will need to look at the individual compatibilities, of which just the Taurean ones are given in this book.

The Taurean Approach to Relationships

A Taurean is wholly motivated by his need to give and receive physical security and reassurance. He has no real sense of his own identity, and does not spend much time thinking about who he is as an abstract idea; he only knows who he is by relating himself to his environment. Reassurance and a sense of worth are achieved by being in welcoming and satisfying surroundings.

It will seem obvious to you, as a Taurean reading this, that if you are not comfortable in your surroundings, then you are not comfortable in general, and will feel that you cannot be at your best until your surroundings are more amenable to your tastes and needs. You also know that unless there is a similar pleasantness in your emotional dealings with the people around you, then you are just as uncomfortable. You cannot imagine things being any other way, but the fact is that only Taureans, and people born with Venus, Taurus' planet, in important places in the sky, do think this way, and the rest of humanity does not.

When you enter a relationship, you want to find all that you can that is common to you and your partner, and make that the basis of your relationship. You do not form relationships by being attracted to people who are nothing like you, striking sparks off each other by parading your differences; you are not strong or secure enough in your views for that. You want them to find parts of you that they like and approve of, and for you to find parts of them that you want to care for in return. It is all to do

with the way that Venus works, always finding the common
ground, and promoting togetherness and unity wherever it can
find a chance to do so. In your case, it is 'collecting' energy (see
pp 12 and 13 if you've forgotten), so you will not be the one to
make the first move. You want to take all the affection that they
feel for you, and keep it for yourself, to be stored up for a rainy
day perhaps. You also want to look after them, and keep them
close to you, so that they will always be there for you to care for,
and to give you the reassurance you need so much. This process
is actually one of acquisition—you are collecting people and
things you care for, and keeping them close to you. It would be
uncharitable, and wrong, to say that you need them exclusively
for your own security: that is only half the story. The energy flow
is nonetheless going into you rather than out of you, though,
and you are definitely benefiting from the affection given to you
by those you love. On the other hand, they need somebody to
give their affection to, and to have that affection so obviously
appreciated is rewarding for them. In addition, they need
security, and you are not the sort of person who is different from
one day to the next; you embody reliability and security for the
rest of the zodiac, and when anybody feels a need to be close to
those qualities because he lacks them himself, he comes to you
to supply them.

What does happen in your relationships is that you become
attached to your partner, and you try to keep them close to you,
as unchanged and stable as you are yourself. This is misinterpreted:
to a lot of people it can seem as though you are trying to stifle
them, stop them growing, and holding them against their will. I
am sure that you would be horrified to think that anyone in a
long-term relationship which was giving you happiness and
emotional nourishment was finding that being loved by you was
smothering them, but you would do well to remember the
possibility of this happening, and make every effort to be
flexible.

You are very sensitive about your emotional state, very easily
wounded, and you carry the hurt for a long time. If it looks as
though your partner wants a little more freedom, you are prone

to interpret this as a criticism of your love for him, and feel wounded. At the same time, you fear that if he leaves you, you will have lost all the reassurance and nourishment you gained, and you start to fight to keep him. You are frightened to let go, and you feel that somebody is taking what's yours, so you cling on harder than before, and refuse to see reason. The situation gets worse. In fact, the situation is irretrievable from here, because you don't know how to release the pressure. Either you lose him and get hurt, or he relents a little to alleviate your worries, thus returning the situation to its pre-crisis state— which will worsen again in due time, because you will not ever see why he feels this way, and will not change your approach. if that makes you sound like a monster, it's not meant to, but it is how you work, and other people find that it needs careful handling.

A relationship which consists of two people who feel emotion- ally secure with each other and share the same needs and fears is what works best for you, and when you have found that, you are much better. Then you put all your energy into building a secure territory for you both, and filling this area with everything which makes your life together more comfortable. This is a long-term project, and you see all relationships this way: each new friendship is potentially a life friendship to you, and you only get into trouble when you encounter people for whom friendship is a temporary diversion, an entertaining episode with no thought of permanence.

You marry, essentially, for security. When you have a home and family around you, you feel that you have the sort of surroundings which are not likely to move around and force you to change direction too frequently. Also, you can play the role of being the centre of the family unit, which you enjoy. You don't want to be just a member of a family, you want to be the centre of the family, so that you can have it around you. As parent, householder, maître d'hôtel, and nurse you can be in control of all the material things that comprise the household. At the same time, you can gain satisfaction from caring for the rest of the family, and receive their appreciation for the way you look after the material side of their existence for them. What your partner has to do is look after you. This is an analogous job to that which the farmer does as he moves the bull from one field to another. It must be done firmly but gently, and the bull must somehow be persuaded that such a move was his intention anyway. It can be a dangerous job.

Individual Compatibilities Sign by Sign

All relationships between the signs work in the ways described earlier in 'How Zodiacal Relationships Work' (page 35). In addition to that, descriptions of how a Taurean attempts to form a relationship with someone from each of the twelve signs are given below. I have tried to show not what a Cancerian, for example, is like, but what a Taurean sees him as, and how he sees you. Each individual Cancerian looks different, of course, but their motivation is the same, and these descriptions are meant to help you understand what you are trying to do with them, and how they are trying to handle you. As usual, the words he and him can be taken to mean she and her, since astrology makes no distinctions in sex here.

Taurus-Aries
All zodiacal partnerships involving adjacent signs are difficult, but this combination is possibly the most difficult of them all. The simple fact is that Arians annoy you. They are worrying to you, and they move much too quickly for you and be able to keep a proper eye on them. You like to know where things are, and where they are going to stay for some time; Arians don't stay anywhere for any length of time, and this is disturbing to you. Perhaps it was their forcefulness that attracted you; you will have discovered that it is not directed towards the defence of their position, as yours is, but towards personal movement. Their energy moves them for movement's sake; you only let yourself be moved when threatened.

They are highly active people, and need to keep busy doing things, whereas you are quite happy to keep things the way they are. This means that while you are at your best staying in one place doing one thing, they are likely to be changing from one thing to another, and you will find it disconcerting. They would like you to be active too, so that they can feel the pleasure of having a partner in action, and they will try to make you move faster than you would really like. Moving too quickly means that you cannot feel the earth under your feet, and this removes you from your element (Earth, remember? Remind yourself with the diagram on page 16). You are naturally frightened to do this, and so refuse to move as quickly as the Arian would like. He sees this as lack of spirit, but does not hold this against you in any way. He must go his own way, and has no time to spend cajoling you into joining him. The fact that you are unwilling, or unable, to join him is a great pity, but can't be helped. It is important for you to understand this—the Arian thinks no worse of you because you won't join in his activities; he simply thinks that it is your loss, and can't be helped. He doesn't feel betrayed, injured, or thwarted in any way. You feel all of these when relationships go wrong, of course; it's part of how you work. He doesn't work like you at all, and that doesn't mean that either of you are wrong, just different. Can you understand that?

Physically, you are well matched, because you both use your bodies as a prime expression of your energies. You will find Arian energy attractive, and would dearly like to be able to keep some of it for later, or to have it for your own. The Arian finds your strength an invigorating test for his sexual capabilities, and on that level at least you should have a lot of excitement and satisfaction. The problems arise when you try to convert the relationship into something steady instead of a momentary passion. The Arian gets bored, and you become possessive. The level of energy in the liaison drops, the sexual excitement fades, and you become more and more determined to hang on to what you see as yours, but which you think is mysteriously being taken away from you. The Arian senses the lack of excitement, the lack of development and novelty as the situation becomes static, and immediately looks for a more interesting project. The result is bound to be disappointment for both of you. There will inevitably be one of those thankfully rare occasions where the Taurean loses his temper in a big way, because he feels that he has somehow been deprived of what was rightfully his.

As a long-term relationship, such as a business or a marriage, this coupling can only work if roles are strictly defined and understood. If that is done, the pressure that you can both bring to bear on problems that beset you can make for a very successful team. The Aries must be allowed to do all the development work, and to do it as his own pace; everything which is untried, or has to be tackled without much preparation, must be left to the Arian. The Taurean must do all the backup work, and be allowed to make it his own territory. He must also convince the Arian that all this effort is worthwhile, by giving patience, the quality the Arian lacks above all; in return, you will be shown that new beginnings are far from impossible when your position really seems hopeless.

Taurus-Taurus
Two bulls in the same field: quite an entertaining proposition for a spectator outside the field, but rather uncomfortable for anyone in the field, and necessarily painful for one, perhaps both, of the bulls.

The relationship is likely to start with some taste that the pair of you have in common: perhaps you like the same sort of food, and enjoy working your way round all the restaurants of that type in your area. Perhaps it is music, or some pastime. Whatever it is, you will be pleased that someone else has the same high opinion of the things that you like as you have. For a Taurean, to have someone give you credit for your tastes is an irresistible compliment to your ego. The same thing, of course is also happening to the other Taurean.

It is easy to get yourself into a sort of race in this situation, where both of you are in competition with the other to have more, or a better one, of whatever it is that you both admire and enjoy possessing. This will last until one of you runs out of money or time. and is fine as far as it goes as long as neither of you take it at all seriously. Both of you will strenuously deny that it *is* at all serious, but it will be so nonetheless, because what you hate most of all is losing—and losing publicly; hence the denials that there is any kind of contest. Both of you like to have just that bit more than the other—whoever first came up with the phrase 'I'll have the big half' was undoubtedly Taurean, and most probably saw nothing funny in what he'd just said.

It is difficult for you to understand the give and take of a relationship at times, because as far as you are concerned you are right. This means that if your partner does something which you disagree with, or, far worse, tries to get you to change your ways, you feel criticized and under attack. There is no reason for you to feel this, but you do nonetheless. If the matter is a small one, you will take no notice, confident that your partner will soon see things your way, and no more need be said. If it is a request for you to do things differently, you simply take no notice, because they are wrong, and that's that. If it is something important, or the requests for unaccustomed action are persistent, then you will wait patiently, and only when the situation becomes intolerable will you move. When you move, you move to re-establish your way of doing things once and for all. Progress and change do not come easily to a Taurean, and an easygoing, patient nature is often just a wounded Taurean hoping that the irritation will go away without having to move. Two people behaving in this way with each other is bound to be difficult. As a marriage, the best thing to do is to find an area about which you both agree very strongly, such as financial growth, or the acquisition of property, and make everything else subordinate to it. This way your personal stubbornnesses become insignificant when you both see how much you have achieved together, and your natural tendencies to keep a good things going if possible will motivate you to settle minor problems for the sake of your greater possessions.

Taurus-Gemini
This partnership is as difficult for you to understand as the Aries one. Fortunately for you, it is nothing like as threatening, and so you can afford to let your differences go by without worrying

about being forced to make changes. You have an appreciation of peace and quiet, of letting the world go by in its own way without interference, which is simply not comprehensible to a Gemini. Their need to think, to read, to receive information and then voice an opinion on it, will occasionally make you wish you could switch them off like a radio. You can't; you will have to live with the noise.

What you find strangest of all with the Gemini is their apparent disregard for things material. If there is food in front of them, they will eat it, but it isn't anything like as important as it is to you. They like a well-appointed house—who doesn't?—but they don't see that as a reflection of themselves and their tastes as you do. What really interests them is a new idea. New information and new developments, the sort of thing you turn your back on in case it heralds change, is the stuff of life to them.

Geminis are the sort of people who think that they are always right, because they have thought about things and come to a definite conclusion. You can appreciate this, because you know that you are right, too; not from thinking about things, but from feeling them, and taking things in slowly. What will surprise and upset you is that a Gemini can change his mind completely every five minutes, and each time he is convinced that he is right. The same mental evaluation has taken place, and the same force of conviction is there, and yet he has changed viewpoint completely. This is very unsettling to you; either he is making it all up, which is potentially threatening to your stability because you may be taken in, or he is right each time, which is worrying because you can't react that fast. If you don't panic, it may dawn on you that this mental evaluation process is actually what he likes doing best, and so he does it as often as he can, continually fascinating himself with the varieties of argument he turns up. As you will realize, all this happens in the world of the imagination and does not affect your position, your territory, or your possessions one bit; you are quite safe, and can let him exercise his imagination to his heart's content. This is why he is less of a threat to your stability than the Arian. Relax, and listen to the chatter; he can be very entertaining indeed once you realize that very little of it is for real.

As lovers, you will be a strange mixture. You would like to have his lightness of touch and his way with words; he makes you feel clumsy and slow, but you find his conversation so flattering, and he makes you feel good. From the other side of the relationship, he needs your stabilizing influence when things aren't going quite the way he'd like them to, which will be a lot more frequently than you would imagine. It's because he never believes that effort is a necessary component of success. You will have to take the role of an understanding parent, while he takes that of the child.

Unless you have strong common interests, it will be difficult to make a lasting partnership from these two signs, because you are not concerned with ideas any more than he is with material things, and he will lose interest in you unless there is something you both enjoy. You must expect arguments from time to time, when he changes his ideas and denies having thought differently before; he must remember that to make his dreams come true requires patience and application, and you are his best source of both those qualities.

Taurus-Cancer

This is a splendid partnership. You are both concerned with the same things in life, but approach them from different, though complementary, directions. Both of you are determined to hang on to what is yours and not to lose things, but you are not in conflict with each other. The important thing from a Cancerian point of view is to have a firm base, to look after what is your own, to care about and make sure that you know about everything that goes on in your territory, and then worry about your responsibilities and your safety. The Taurean point of view is nothing like so frantic; to make sure that your territory stays yours is all; being recognized as the owner is a welcome bonus.

The Cancerian worries too much about things, whereas the Taurean trusts his own abilities and is of the opinion that if nothing is done to upset the general arrangement of things, nothing drastic will happpen. The Cancerian isn't so sure, and it is here that the relationship starts to work: the Cancerian comes to the Taurean for advice and reassurance about matters of security, knowing that he isn't going to sound silly. In return, the Taurean knows that if he wants somebody to share his possessions and his taste for the good life without getting involved in a game of one-upmanship or a situation that threatens his position, then the sensitive Cancerian is just the one. Like a younger sister, the Cancerian is mildly envious of all that the Taurean has managed to collect, and appreciates being allowed to use some of it. She may not agree completely with her big sister's taste, but she is far too reserved, and too aware of what's good for her in the long run, to voice any criticism.

Cancerians are quite capable of expanding their responsibilities and the areas under their control, and often do. They are prepared to do something completely new if they feel that it is in their best interest. It is not usual to call them adventurous, but in comparison to the Taurean, who will always take the tried and trusted method rather than risk anything unfamiliar, it can seem that way. Certainly a Cancerian is more motivated to advance his ambitions into new fields than the Taurean; but, having got there, he feels responsible for all the people under him and is unable to simply to pass over them. It's not a territorial urge so much as a caring and almost parenting feeling, but it is one which a Taurean understands at once.

Home is important to a Cancerian, because it is his personal caring environment. It needs to be secure, and it needs to be comfortable. Taureans are very fond of lavishly appointed homes, and so any home that you share together will be of great importance to you, and you will both work hard to make it as comfortable and welcoming as possible, if for slightly different reasons.

As lovers, you will be very affectionate, very caring and very understanding, through the physical electricity that the Fire signs like Aries and Sagittarius brings to a relationship will be missing. Earth and Fire are a lightning strike, after all, whereas what we have here is Earth and Water, producing a fertile environment. That works in all ways— Earth and Water people together have large and happy families.

As a marriage, the arrangement seems perfect. If there is a flaw, it may be that eventually you become so set in your ways and so home-centred that you feel a need for something else to do; but taken as a whole the marriage is unlikely to develop any more serious problems than obesity as the two of you indulge your liking for food and the security it represents.

Taurus-Leo

This is an interesting pairing—almost interesting enough to sell tickets to watch. Two powerful animals, A Bull and a Lion, both used to being their own master, and unaccustomed to giving way on anything, attempting to make an equal relationship. If it succeeds, and there will be a few broken plates before it settles down, then it will be very strong indeed, and a union which will bring great material wealth and prestige to its partners.

The essential conflict is something similar to ignoring a 'Do Not Walk On The Grass' notice under the park-keeper's nose. A Taurean has a very acute sense of his own territory, and will have things done according to his wishes within that territory. Trespassers or people refusing to recognize his authority within that territory are seen as threats. So far, so good. A Leo, however, regards himself as the natural authority figure and centre of attention wherever he happens to be, and will behave in the firm belief that this is indeed so. He also feels free to go wherever the mood takes him, so long as he has an opportunity to display his personal warmth and radiance to a suitable audience. When he strides into the Taurean's territory he will expect appreciation and respect, and be hurt not to receive it; almost as hurt as the Taurean is by the lack of recognition he is afforded by the Leo. Neither of them is of the sort likely to smile and forget. They will insist on recognition, and because they are both fixed signs (page 15) they will not bend an inch away from what they think is theirs. Such arguments can lead to separations lasting years; the families which don't speak to each other for generations are showing this fixed sign behaviour.

The way for a Taurean to achieve some measure of understanding with a Leo is for the Leo to handle the theory and the

Taurean to handle the practicalities. If they agree on the same goals, then the Leo can provide a way for the Taurean to display his wealth without seeming offensive (everybody likes Leos, and expects them to be rich; not everybody likes a wealthy Taurean), while the Taurean generates more wealth from the opportunities the Leo provides. If this is done, a partnership capable of generating very large amounts of money is created, provided you limit yourselves to doing what you know best, and don't branch out into the new and unfamiliar.

As lovers you will be devoted to each other, and enjoy taking your territorial struggles to the bedroom; you will both be strong, but a little conventional, in your approaches to sex. As a Taurean you will have to be ready for a few tall stories from your Leo lover, and don't be surprised if this continues in the pub. Leos are the best in the world; they know it, and they tell everybody so when they get an audience. Everybody loves them for it, and nobody cares whether any of it is true or not.

As marriage partners you will be very loyal to each other, and fight on each other's behalf when necessary; you will build a home and family life which becomes richer and more plentiful as time goes on. You will have to learn that Leos are easily hurt if they think that you don't care much for some of their ideas, and you will have to develop a way of letting them down gently using that Taurean patience. You will be needlessly possessive; they are as loyal to you as you to them. They will have to learn that at home, particularly, you are the boss; you are unlikely to teach them, or spell it out for them, so they must learn it on their own. Sometimes they are as slow to accept the unpalatable as you are, so give them time to get used to the idea.

Taurus-Virgo
This partnership can work very well. You are both Earth signs, and so you are both interested in using your energy in the same general way. You may find the Virgoan fussy, though, and they will almost certainly find you rather hefty and careless in your approach to many things.

The essential thing about a Virgoan's approach to life is

getting the details right. It matters to them that they have the right way of going about things; often they will find enjoyment and satisfaction in a repetitive job, because to them each time is different, and they are continually learning and re-learning their technique. 'Practice' is a very Virgoan word. They like things to feel good, and are much happier when they can feel and touch things for themselves. They modify whatever they own, changing little bits of it here and there to make it that little bit neater, or a closer fit, or whatever.

To you, this obsession with detail is strange. You can understand the care and attention that is lavished on belongings, because you feel strongly about that too, but the constant search for perfection baffles you. You do not like to change your way of doing something; you only learn it once, and however sloppy you become after that, you still believe that you are doing it in the same way, and will not be persuaded otherwise. The Virgoan is never sloppy; his technique is always up to the mark, and constantly in practice, because he analyses what he does as he does it. He analyses what he is about to do before he does it. He thinks about how he would analyse it before he has to. As a result, he makes the best possible use of all the material at hand, and you seem to him to be unthinking in your use of your talents. You seem not to consider how best to do something, only whether to do it. You seem not to consider how to adapt something to fit you better, only how to acquire it. Above all, you seem not to care what it is that you have, only to care that you have it, and that other people recognize this. The area in which you come closest to each other is in that of selection, where you both pick the best you can, and reject the rest—one on the grounds of flavour, the other on the grounds of excellence of function.

In many ways, you wish you could be as careful and as perceptive as the Virgo; you feel that your life could be considerably enriched by his knowledge and insight, and his knowledge of correct technique would save you from making a fool of yourself on numerous occasions. For his part, he wishes he could simply command as much as you do; what couldn't he do if he didn't have to spend his time working on such a small scale—and imagine having the confidence and wealth to be careless with it all! Your immovable presence and authority, your appreciation of material comforts, is an inspiration to a Virgo, while his skills and insight are all that you would like to be, but can't be bothered ever to strive to become.

As lovers, you will have to be gentle and easy in your approach; Virgos are delicate creatures, and are easy to trample. Try to be considerate and careful; take time over details. In return, he will have to realize that your big gestures of affection are not at all clumsy or uncaring, but genuine declarations of affection on a rather bigger scale than he thinks is proper. He must restrain himself from telling you how to do things better, which is only a mask for his insecurity (a Taurean in love is a bit too forceful for him to deal with in small sections, as he would like).

As a marriage prospect, these signs are better than most of the same-element pairings. The constantly active nature of the Virgoan will stop things from ever being too much the same, and will work hard to make all as good as it can possibly be. Let him use you as a protector and defender against his enemies and fears, whilst you use him to help you get the very best use out of whatever it is that you have achieved. Not only will you have your own bit of land, but it will have the neatest, prettiest and most fruitful garden you have ever seen!

Taurus-Libra

A very happy partnership, this, because both of you are motivated and directed by the planet Venus, which looks for points of common interest, and tries to promote friendship and harmony. So not only are you pleased to meet somebody else who has a similar motivation to you, but you actually like them, too; what's more, they like you in return, and that is always a good sign in a relationship.

Librans have a distinctive talent for saying the right thing at the right time, and adding little touches here and there which make things easy on the eye. They can see at once what needs doing to make a room beautiful, and will do it without fuss, just to please themselves. A Libran home is always refined and beautiful, but pleasant to be in as well, which might not always be the case were other signs to be the homebuilders. They have the same simple elegance in their clothes; whatever they wear looks just right. Even their speech is pleasant. There is always something about the way a Libran does things that makes others think 'I wish I could be like that!'

As a Taurean, you appreciate beautiful things, and you like to be near them. The attraction of a person who is in themselves beautiful and graceful is not hard to see. From the other side, they see you as offering the sort of appreciation they like, and feel that they could form a close and rewarding relationship with someone who shares their view of life. A Libran is always trying to form relationships, make friends, gather people close to him; the problem lies in the sad fact that many people do not share his aesthetic view of things, are unreliable or discourteous, disloyal even. All these things upset the exact balance of the Libran existence and cause disharmony, which he feels strongly. He knows that he can always rely on the Taurean to be constant, loyal, and unchanging; that, coupled with the Taurean sense of admiration for all things which are beautiful to look at, makes for a friendship which is especially valuable to the Libran. You restore him when the world seems to be over-demanding, harsh, and unrefined. Through you, he knows that his essential values of harmony and quiet co-existence are still worth pursuing, and are constant despite temporary indications to the contrary. He needs no training in artistic sensibilities, but he does need strength, and he has to look for it outside himself. You can offer that in abundance, and he will give you in return the grace and charm that you sometimes feel you lack.

You may feel in the initial stages of your friendship that the Libran is too cool. This is not so, but they are certainly light in their approach to things, and the airy delicacy of their way of conducting an affair may seem insubstantial to you. From their point of view, you will seem heavy and a little lacking in subtlety. They will also find you short of originality, and a slow talker. Librans are from an Air sign, remember, and they need to circulate ideas. They also need to circulate amongst people, so don't keep them indoors, and don't get upset if they like talking to everybody else at a party. They'll come back. Remember that this social circulation is as important to them as eating is to you. Do you want them to starve to death? Take things on a light level if you can, and keep the relationship mobile.

As lovers you might have to be very understanding with each other. The Libran will find your passion and strength a little overwhelming, and lacking in refinement; you will find his preference for love and romance rather than sex delightful to begin with but frustrating later. Don't get upset if he runs away, but make sure that he realizes that it is important to you just the same.

As marriage partners you should be amusing to watch. Both of you are very particular about your home environment, and you will have it beautifully furnished, but neither of you will want to do much about its upkeep, because you are both quite lazy given half a chance. You will eat the most exquisite meals in the grandest style, but neither of you will want to wash up afterwards. You will have not only to take responsibility for the house, but some of the actual work involved too, and the Libran will have to accept his share as well. 'Share' is a Libran word—the idea of equal chores and equal responsibility is one which makes a lot of sense to his Airy mind, and has enough practicality built in to keep your Taurean needs satisfied too.

Taurus-Scorpio

A powerful thing, the meeting of two signs opposed to each other in the circle of the zodiac, especially when they are both fixed signs. You can expect them to be just as determined to have their own way as you are, and just as hard to move in any way they feel is not quite right for them. You can expect them to be able to do all the things that you can't, but there again, you can do all the things that they can't, so you end up even. All this sounds ominous, but you have quite a lot in common, and won't find it too difficult to get on with one another provided you have enough room for the pair of you not to feel threatened by each other.

You like to be in control of your physical environment, as you know well. This means that you like to know what's yours, and what comes into, or goes on in, or goes out of, your little bit of space. It is your field, and you are the bull in that field. A Scorpio likes to be in control of his emotional environment. This means that he likes to know how he feels, and how everybody else's actions and feelings are likely to affect his own. In turn, this means that he has to look into things to see how they work and what's going on, because unless he is fully up to date with all the possibilities, he may not be able to maintain his control over how he feels. You have an easier job of it, really; possessions don't change as fast as feelings. You may feel that you have more than a little of the Scorpio in you, now that you have read about what he's trying to do; many Scorpios will feel that they have more than a little of the Taurean in them, too. They usually like having things which remind them of how in control they are, like powerful cars.

The difference between the two of you, apart from the difference between possessions and feelings, is the difference between maintenance and control. A Scorpio isn't trying to maintain his feelings in the same state; he's trying to control them, so that they do what he wants. You're not trying to control your territory; you're trying to maintain it, so that it stays more or less as it is, but improving all the while. There is quite a difference.

You will be able to see at once that if the two of you are placed too close to each other, you will both feel threatened. So powerful and strongly controlled an individual on your territory is obviously unsettling to you, especially as you seem to be unable to see what he's thinking, and are afraid that he might take something from you; on his side, he is bothered by your immovability and apparent imperturbability, which could make you difficult to control, and have a possibly upsetting influence on his feelings. Given a little distance, you will both be able to see that your areas of concern may overlap but they do not intersect, and so you need have nothing to fear from each other.

As friends and partners, you could make a great deal of money together, because you represent the signs which are concerned with the effective use of all kinds of resources, financial included. Provided you have one person to do the organizing, and one to look after the stock, you will make an effective team. You might suffer from being a little on the dull side, since neither of you are originators of new ideas, but the Scorpio's assiduous research capabilities should ensure that you keep up with new developments in business as soon as somebody else has tested them and found that they work.

As lovers, you will express yourselves very powerfully indeed, but you will find that the emotional intensity with which the Scorpio conducts his love affairs will make your Taurean head feel dizzy. You like things powerful, sure, but you like them relaxed and easy-going, too; the constant atmosphere of almost obsessive passion will leave you gasping for air. Still, if you can stand that sort of thing, you won't feel that it isn't strong enough for you, as you might have done with the Libran, for example.

As marriage partners, the same thing applies. You both want success and security, and as a couple you should have no problems in achieving these goals. When you've got all that, though, you want to sit back in relative tranquillity and enjoy it all, whereas the Scorpio is driven to do more and more. Basically, they never stop, where you feel that resting after your labours is important as the work itself. If you can live with his constant determination to achieve more, without feeling irritated or criticized yourself, then fine.

Taurus-Sagittarius

These two signs are very different. They seem to get in each other's way more often than not when they act together, but when they stand back and look at the other in action they can each see what the other is trying to achieve. The Fire of the Sagittarian seems to scorch and wither all that the Taurean has worked so hard to achieve, while the Taurean seems too much of a plodder to appreciate the brilliance and verve of the Archer. There are other ways to look at it, though; the Taurean can provide a solid home base for the Sagittarian to come back to when he is in one of his crestfallen phases, and the Sagittarian can provide the optimism and insight that Taurean folk often cannot find in themselves. It takes effort from both sides to achieve that, though, and there must be a strong motivation for other reasons to keep the relationship together long enough for that kind of rapport to grow.

Think of the two animals from the signs, the bull and the horse. The bull lives in his own field, and doesn't move far from it; the horse leaps over the fence, and is soon away into the far distance, running with the wind for its own sake (an important thing to understand about Sagittarians—the need to be free and the joy of doing things for their own sake out of curiosity). The horse is more beautiful when in motion, the bull more majestic when standing still. Horses are essentially a luxury item, whereas cattle are much more useful in terms of what they produce. You can perhaps begin to see that the signs do not have a great deal to offer one another.

Having a Sagittarian friend is a disturbing experience for a Taurean. They seem to move so quickly; you take life at a steadier pace where you can, and dislike being rushed. They concentrate so much on intellectual things—ideas and concepts which have no real foundation or practical application, things they read in books. One minute they are on about one thing as though it was the only thing in the world, and the next minute it's something else altogether. Never the same twice. If you thought about it for a moment, you would see that they answer the deepest questions for you—questions so deep that you might never think of asking them. You might ask yourself, as you go through life looking after and assimilating your belongings, whether there was more, and where it might come from. The Sagittarian answers you. He shows you endless realms, shows you new things coming into being as ideas, and being translated into action and form. He is a creator, and you are a collector: the relationship is a deep one, and not often questioned or examined in daily life, but there it is.

He sees you as the sort of result his ideas must eventually be seen as. After all, he is trying to make things happen; if he succeeds, then the planetary energy will be collected into one place, and become Earth where it was once Fire. Besides, without the wealth of material you offer, not only in terms of money, but also in terms of effort, loyalty, and patience, then he can achieve nothing. On a personal level, he sees you as slow and rather predictable, but he is more than a little envious of your patience and the steadiness you seem to bring to life. He would not seriously trade the roller-coaster of emotional ups and downs he lives on, but when you don't like what you have at the moment a little of the opposite always seems attractive . . .

As lovers, you would be a lot more successful physically than you might have thought, but the rest of the relationship would need a lot of work. The trouble is that you need to feel that a person belongs to you, and you to them; a Sagittarian belongs to himself and to nobody else, and if you start to get possessive, then he will gallop off and find somebody else. Even when he is pledged to you (and he is, if he says so; they never lie) he will still entertain himself with new acquaintances of the opposite sex; variety and games are very important and restorative to him. Having the same thing all the time makes him depressed. He will choose to come back to you quite freely, but he can never be compelled to do so. Being totally loyal to him doesn't really count; he sees you as a millstone then. A Sagittarian really does need to be allowed to go his own way; trap him and his fire dies, which is useless if what you were trying to do was keep his warmth for your own private use.

As marriage partners, you will have to make allowances for their need to move around, and make sure that you give them both the space and the opportunity to use it. He will need to realize that you need a base to return to, which is permanently and unchangeably yours. If you are married to a Sagittarian, or are considering it, then you must already have found some other interest which is strong enough to hold you both together. Without that joint interest and goal, you will need to put in what is probably more effort than you would like to make the relationship really work.

Taurus-Capricorn

This is the relationship that's built to last. Two Earth signs, one fixed and one cardinal, both interested in making things firm, secure, and unchanging, and both with a fondness for things of enduring value—here is the recipe for a life partnership. It might be a little slow to get started, because both of you will be quite secure in your own areas, and will see no reason to interrupt things to allow the entry of someone new and possibly threatening to you; when you see how similar you are to each other you will start to like each other, and things will grow from there.

This is the four-signs-apart relationship, the mutual admiration society where each partner wishes he were more like the other one. In this particular case, the Taurean is probably impressed by the way that the Capricorn seems to get recognition and respect for all that he has achieved, and is seen as a natural and obvious winner in life. Taureans would like to have acclaim and recognition for their efforts, and it is the hope of this that motivates them anew when they are despondent. They also appreciate and approve of the way a Capricorn measures his success in material terms, or in the way that the world in general thinks of as showing that he's made it in life. Sometimes Taureans get a little confused by people from the other elements who don't seem to value bricks and mortar to the same extent that they do; but then along comes a Capricorn who both reassures and encourages the Taureans, and confidence is restored. This is an important process: fixed signs do not like to feel insecure in any way, and need reassurance from time to time. For a Taurean, a Capricorn is the answer.

From the other point of view, the Capricorn finds the Taurean solidity and determination the perfect expression of the work ethic so central to his way of seeing things. In point of fact, Capricorns are just the faintest bit lazy. It is a very faint bit, agreed, but it is there, and it shows in that they will work and work to achieve something they have set their hearts on, but against determined and repeated opposition they will give up and aim themselves towards something else. If you think for a few minutes you can see why: the need of the Capricorn is to feel achievement, and if things look like being unattainable then an alternative target may give them that sense of achievement sooner. A Taurean takes opposition as a personal affront, and stays where he is until he has worn the opposition down. The Capricorn thinks this is admirable. Working hard for high rewards he can understand, but working patiently and unceasingly with no guarantee of having the work recognized, as the Taurean often does, strikes the Capricorn as an almost saintly devotion to the cause, and he is lost in admiration.

As a friendship or business partnership, of course, this pairing has a lot to offer; the Taurean can share in the Capricorn's achievements as reward for his efforts, and the Capricorn can aim even higher for the pair of you in the knowledge that the Taurean will never deviate from the job in hand, no matter how difficult progress becomes. You will need to have somebody else around to provide both of you with new directions and ideas from time to time, or you will become rather dull and unimaginative, but otherwise there is a lot to recommend this as a business partnership.

As lovers, there will be many power games for the two of you to amuse yourselves with, but the cool Capricorn does not understand the nature of real passion, and his response to your Taurean physical needs may not be enough. You will have to show him that physical contact and being touched are important to you, and invite him to express himself in a similar way. He'll never quite get it right, but he can be persuaded to join in to a certain extent.

As a marriage, this partnership looks good. Your tastes are different, though; you like things soft, pretty and luxurious, with plenty of food available—the Capricorn often doesn't care what or when he eats. Some of them are very flashy dressers, though; if you can find one of these, you will have a further point of contact through your love of colour and texture, and this will help you build a comfortable home together.

Taurus-Aquarius
This match isn't easy at all. To put it simply, they feel safest in a

crowd, whereas you feel safest at home; they are better with lots of people at once, and you are better in a one-to-one relationship.

You would think that somebody who was of the opposite sign to you in the zodiac would be opposite to you in every way, but that is not in fact the case. What happens is that the two people concerned are at odds because they are in so many ways similar rather than different. It is here, where the polarity of the signs is different, where the two of you are three signs apart, that the real differences emerge. You are dedicated to the maintenance of what's yours; you have worked for it, you are going to keep it, and you want everybody to respect you for the efforts you have put into its acquisition. An Aquarian is dedicated, in just the same way, to the breakdown of all structures which imply that anybody is better than, or higher than, anybody else. Difficult to imagine, isn't it?

Why were you attracted to him in the first place? It may well have been the fact that he always has so many friends, and is so popular. You become part of the audience, find that the group is a generally happy one, and enjoy the companionship and appreciation you get from other members of the group. Then you project yourself towards the group's centre (or, as Taureans do, charge like a bull) and acquire him. Now you can become possessive with him—he is yours. Unfortunately, he is not going to see it your way. He is not going to understand the depth of your feelings, your need to hold on to what you have, your need to be appreciated. You are not going to understand why he still needs to have a hundred friends when he has you.

Aquarians like to be different. More than that, they need to be different. Whenever they see something that has been established the way it is for some considerable time and is doing quite nicely, thank you, they feel that it is time for a change, and so they disturb, rearrange, and sometimes destroy things. It is not from a sense of malice, or even one of mischievous glee: it is simply the way they are built. They represent the idea that everything has its time, and at the end of that time it must change. Change is then a natural state for them, and the movement and conversation which flows round groups of people is an environment as natural and healthy for them as your home is for you. Being static is an unhealthy thing for them; collecting things which are going to last seems absurd, because they are dedicated to the concept of change.

It would seem that there could be no contact between you, but in fact there is a genuine attraction of opposites. He is interested in the nature of constancy simply because it is alien to him, and you represent that; you are interested in the nature of change, because it shows you the world outside your own experience, and fascinates you because you know you wouldn't like to live in it for long. Perhaps you both recognize that you are different aspects of the same thing. Whatever changes is still itself, but in a different form; whatever is formed must change in time, like the seasons. You will be strong in each other's defence, and yet equally strong in maintaining your differences within the relationship.

As lovers, you are bound to have difficulties because of the differences between Taurean possessiveness and Aquarian freedom. Physically, he will be inventive and adventurous, which will excite you, yet emotionally rather uninvolved, which could make you feel betrayed. In turn, he will find your passion and devotion rewarding, though its persistence and occasionally demanding nature will make him slip out from under from time to time to see other people and feel refreshed in their company.

If a marriage is to be built out of this relationship, you will both have to compromise to a large extent; his more revolutionary and far-ranging ideas will have to be shelved, and you must offer him some sort of willingnes to adopt changes from time to time. Shared interests will help—both of you like music as a rule, though it may not be the same kind, of course.

Taurus-Pisces
Here is the relationship you have been waiting for, where you hardly ever have to show your horns, and you can give yourself almost completely to a life of relaxation and softness, self-indulgent for both you and your partner.

You are both just what the other one needs. The softer side of you—that which, given a chance, would spend its time in pursuit of elegance, artistry, and gracious living—finds the romantic and impressionistic approach of the Piscean very easy to accommodate. They are supremely sensitive individuals, and will adapt themselves to anything which comes their way. They are refined, and fond of luxury if they can get it; your strong point of view and determined way of doing things are more than enough guidance for them, while your own tastes are much along the same lines as their own. There should be very few disagreements.

You often feel yourself to be a little dull mentally, and wish that you could be as intellectual as some of the other signs. At the same time, you are wary of the harsh brilliance of the Gemini's wit, or the simply overwhelming erudition of the Sagittarian mind. Perhaps there is a softer mind, a gentler imagination, to which you might aspire? The Piscean has exactly that, and will help you develop your own imagination in the best possible way.

The softness of the Piscean is no threat to you, and you will seldom have to fight to get your own way. Most of the time you won't notice that they have any opinion different from yours at all. You will also enjoy looking after them, and loving them, because they are so delicate where you are strong, and so very appreciative of any kindness shown to them.

From the Piscean point of view, you are the sort of firm, no-nonsense individual that he needs to put some sort of shape and organization into his life, but without being bossy. He recognizes that he is not able to take assertive action by himself and needs guidance, but he is afraid that any such guide might be insensitive to his feelings, and unappreciative of what he has to offer. In the Taurean he knows that he has the perfect answer: someone strong, determined, and purposeful, but very caring, very patient, and very sensitive at the same time. In return for having his life put into manageable order, the Piscean offers heightened sensitivity and understanding on all matters to do with the emotional response to life, and an unmatched imagination —plus the ability to escape into fantasy and self-comforting whenever life becomes too depressing!

As friends you should be constant, forgiving of each other's little excesses, and very fond of each other. It is not a relationship with which to go out and achieve things; it is much more a restorative retreat for two people who can get easily bruised in the outside world, and need a little care and attention in their private life to redress the balance.

As lovers, your relationship should be very romantic indeed, but you may be surprised and confused from time to time because they are not as direct as you, and do things in rather vague and difficult-to-grasp ways. Be patient: they are not being devious, just vague. Try not to be heavy-handed in your demands. They love you dearly, but they just don't have the physical needs that you do.

As a marriage, this pairing should work very very well, provided that somebody takes responsibility for something somewhere. It's probably best if you make the decisions and they abide by them. You're more sensible.

Part 3

Your Life

5. The Year within Each Day

You have probably wondered, in odd moments, why there are more than twelve varieties of people. You know more than twelve people who look completely different. You also know more than one person with the same Sun sign as yourself who doesn't look anything like you. You also know two people who look quite like each other, but who are not related, and do not have birthdays near each other, so can't be of the same Sun sign. You will have come to the conclusion that Sun signs and astrology don't work too well, because anyone can see that there are more than twelve sorts of people.

You will also have wondered, as you finished reading a newspaper or magazine horoscope, how those few sentences manage to apply to a twelfth of the nation, and why it is that they are sometimes very close to your true circumstances, and yet at other times miles off. You will have come to the conclusion that astrology isn't all that it might be, but some of it is, and that you like it enough to buy magazines for the horoscopes, and little books like this one.

It might be that there is some other astrological factor, or factors, which account for all the different faces that people have, the similarities between people of different Sun signs, and the apparent inconsistencies in magazine horoscopes. There are, indeed, lots of other astrological factors we could consider, but one in particular will answer most of the inconsistencies we have noticed so far.

It is the Ascendant, or rising sign. Once you know your Ascendant, you will see how you get your appearance, your way of working, your tastes, your preferences and dislikes, and your state of health (or not, as the case may be). It is perhaps of more use to you to consider yourself as belonging to your Ascendant sign, than your Sun sign. You have been reading the wrong newspaper horoscopes for years; you are not who you thought you were!

You are about to protest that you know when your birthday is. I'm sure you do. This system is not primarily linked to your birthday, though. It is a smaller cogwheel in the clockwork of the heavens, and we must come down one level from where we have been standing to see its movements. Since astrology is basically the large patterns of the sky made small in an individual, there are a number of 'step-down' processes where the celestial machinery adjusts itself to the smaller scale of mankind; this is one of them.

Here's the theory:

Your birthday pinpoints a particular time during the year. The Sun appears to move round the strip of sky known as the zodiac during the course of the year. In reality, of course, our planet, Earth, moves round the Sun once a year, but the great friendly feature of astrology is that it always looks at things from our point of view; so, we think we stand still, and the Sun appears to move through the zodiac. On a particular day of importance, such as your birthday, you can see which of the zodiac signs the Sun is in, pinpoint how far it has gone in its annual trip round the sky, and then say 'This day is important to me, because it is my birthday; therefore this part of the sky is important to me because the Sun is there on my special day. What are the qualities of that part of the Sun's journey through the zodiac, and what are they when related to me?' The answer is what you usually get in a horoscope book describing your Sun sign.

Fine. Now let's go down one level, and get some more detail. The Earth rotates on its own axis every day. This means that, from our point of view, we stand still and the sky goes round us once a day. Perhaps you hadn't thought of it before, but that's how the Sun appears to move up and across the sky from sunrise to sunset. It's actually us who are moving, but we see it the other way round. During any day, then, your birthday included, the whole of the sky goes past you at some time or another; but at a particular moment of importance, such as the time that you were born, you can see where the Sun is, see which way up the sky is, and say, 'This moment is important to me, because I was born at this time; therefore the layout of the sky has the same qualities as I do. What are the qualities of the sky at this time of day, and what are they when related to me?'

You can see how you are asking the same questions one level lower down. The problem is that you don't know which bit of the sky is significant. Which bit do you look at? All you can see? All that you can't (it's spherical from your point of view, and has no joins; half of it is below the horizon, remember)?

How about directly overhead? A very good try; the point in the zodiac you would arrive at is indeed significant, and is used a lot by astrologers, but there is another one which is more useful still. The eastern horizon is the point used most. Why? Because it fulfils more functions than any other point. It gives a starting point which is easily measurable, and is even visible (remember, all astrology started from observations made before mathematics or telescopes). It is also the contact point between the sky and the earth, from our point of view, and thus symbolizes the relationship between the sky and mankind on the earth. Finally, it links the smaller cycle of the day to the larger one of the year, because the Sun starts its journey on the eastern horizon each day as it rises; and, if we are concerned with a special moment, such as the time of your birth, then the start of the day, or the place that it started, at any rate, is analogous to the start of your life. Remember that you live the qualities of the moment you were born for all of your life; you are that moment made animate.

The point in the zodiac, then, which was crossing the eastern horizon at the time you were born, is called the Ascendant. If this happened to be somewhere in the middle of Gemini, then you have a Gemini Ascendant, or Gemini rising, whichever phrase you prefer. You will see that this has nothing to do with the time

Different signs are on the horizon at different times according to where you live, as you can see. This is because of the difference in latitude. If you live in between the places given, you can make a guess from the values here. To compensate for longitude, subtract twelve minutes from your birthtime if you live in Glasgow, Liverpool or Cardiff; ten minutes for Edinburgh or Manchester, and six minutes for Leeds, Tyneside, or the West Midlands. *Add* four minutes for Norwich.

of year that you were born, only with the time of day.

Have a look at the diagrams on page 70, which should help explain things. If two people are born on the same day, but at different times, then the Ascendant will be different, and the Sun and all the other planets will be occupying different parts of the sky. It makes sense to assume, then, that they will be different in a number of ways. Their lives will be different, and they will look different. What they will have in common is the force of the Sun in the same sign, but it will show itself in different ways because of the difference in time and position in the sky.

How do you know which sign was rising over the eastern horizon when you were born? You will have to work it out. In the past, the calculation of the Ascendant has been the subject of much fuss and secrecy, which astrologers exploit to the full, claiming that only they can calculate such things. It does take some doing, it is true, but with a few short cuts and a calculator it need only take five minutes.

Here is the simplest routine ever devised for you to calculate your own Ascendant, provided that you know your time of birth. Pencil your answers alongside the stages as you go, so you know where you are.

1. Count forwards from 20 April to your birthday: 20 April is 1, 21 April is 2, and so on.
   Total days: . . . .

2. Add 212 to this. New total is: . . . .

3. Divide by 365, and then

4. Multiply by 24. Answer is now: . . . .
   (Your answer by now is between 0 and 24. If it isn't, you have made a mistake somewhere. Go back and try again.)

5. Add your time of birth, in 24-hour clock time. If you were born at 3 p.m., that means 15. If you were born in Summer Time, take one hour off. If there are some spare minutes, your calculator would probably like them in decimals, so it's 0.1 of an hour for each six minutes. 5.36 p.m. is 17.6, for example. Try to be as close as you can. New total is: . . . .

6. If your total exceeds 24, subtract 24. Your answer must now be between 0 and 24. Answer is: . . . .

7. You have now got the time of your birth not in clock time, but in sidereal, or star, time, which is what astrologers work in. Page 70 has a strip diagram with the signs of the zodiac arranged against a strip with the values 0 to 24, which are hours in star time. Look against the time you have just calculated, and you will see which sign was rising at the time you were born. For example, if your calculated answer is 10.456, then your Ascendant is about the 16th degree of Scorpio.

What Does the Ascendant Do?

Broadly speaking, the Ascendant does two things. Firstly, it gives you a handle on the sky, so that you know which way up it was at the time you entered the game, so to speak; this has great significance later on in the book, when we look at the way you handle large areas of activity in your life such as your career, finances, and ambitions. Secondly, it describes your body. If you see your Sun sign as your mentality and way of thinking, then your Ascendant sign is your body and your way of doing things. Think of your Sun sign as the true you, but the Ascendant as the vehicle you have to drive through life. It is the only one you have, so you can only do with it the things of which it is capable, and there may be times when you would like to do things in a different way, but it 'just isn't you'. What happens over your life is that your Sun sign energies become specifically adapted to express themselves to their best via your Ascendant sign, and you become an amalgam of the two. If you didn't, you would soon become very ill. As a Taurean with, say, a Cancer Ascendant, you do things from a Taurean motivation, but in a Cancer way, using a Cancer set of talents and abilities, and a Cancer body. The next few sections of the book explain what this means for each of the Sun/Ascendant combinations.

Some note ought to be made of the correspondence between the Ascendant and the actual condition of the body. Since the

Ascendant sign represents your physical frame rather than the personality inside it, then the appearance and well-being of that frame is also determined by the Ascendant sign. In other words, if you have a Libra Ascendant, then you should look like a Libran, and you should be subject to illnesses in the parts of the body with a special affinity to that sign.

The Astrology of Illness

This is worth a book in itself, but it is quite important to say that the astrological view of illness is that the correlation between the individual and the larger universe is maintained. In other words, if you continue over a long period of time with a way of behaviour that denies the proper and necessary expression of your planetary energies, then the organ of your body which normally handles that kind of activity for your body systems will start to show the stresses to you. A simple example: Gemini looks after the lungs, which circulate air, and from which oxygen is taken all over the body. Gemini people need to circulate among a lot of people, talking and exchanging information. They act as the lungs of society, taking news and information everywhere. They need to do this to express their planetary energies, and society needs them to do this or it is not refreshed, and does not communicate. You need your lungs to do this, too. Lungs within people, Geminis within society: same job, different levels. If you keep a Gemini, or he keeps himself, through circumstance or ignorance, in a situation where he cannot talk or circulate, or where he feels that his normal status is denied, then he is likely to develop lung trouble. This need not be anything to do with a dusty atmosphere, or whether he smokes, although obviously neither of those will help; they are external irritants, and this is an internal problem caused by imbalance in the expression of the energies built into him since birth. In the sections which follow, all the observations on health are to do with how the body shows you that certain behaviour is unbalancing you and causing unnecessary stress; problems from these causes are alleviated by listening to yourself and changing your behaviour.

Your Ascendant

Aries Ascendant

If you have Aries rising, you are an uncommon individual, because Aries only rises for about fifty minutes out of the twenty-four hour day. You must have been born an hour or so before sunrise, or else you have got your sums wrong somewhere.

What you are trying to do with yourself is project a Taurean personality through an Arian vehicle. You will always be trying to do things faster than anybody else, and this can lead to hastiness and a certain degree of accident-proneness. What you see as the correct way to do things involves immediate action by the most direct method, to secure instant, and measurable, results. You feel that unless you are directly and personally responsible for doing things, then they cannot be done, not only because you believe that only you can do them properly, but because you get no satisfaction from letting anybody else do anything. Personal experience of everything is the only way you learn; reading about it, or watching it, does nothing for you.

You are likely to have headaches as a recurring problem if you push yourself too hard, and you should watch your blood pressure too. Mars, ruling Aries, is a strong and forceful planet, and it is bound to get you a little over-stressed at times. You are also likely to have problems digesting things properly. Astrologically, all illnesses apply to your external condition as well as your internal condition, so think carefully; when your head aches you are banging it too hard against a problem which cannot be overcome that way, and when you are not digesting properly, you have not understood the implications of what you have taken on. In both cases, allow time to think and consider.

Taurus Ascendant

You were born at about sunrise if you have Taurus rising as well as a Taurus Sun. You are a double Taurean, doing things in a Taurean way, and with a Taurean body as your vehicle as well. You should have all the Taurean physical characteristics: quite thick-set, big around the neck and shoulders sometimes, and with large hands. You should have a broad mouth, and large eyes, which are very attractive. You should also have a good voice—not only as a singing voice, but one which is pleasant to listen to in conversation too.

The Taurean method for getting things done is to look forward to, and then enjoy, the material reward for one's efforts. It is part of Taurean thinking that if you can't touch it, buy it, own it or eat it, it isn't real and it isn't worth much. You will also be concerned to keep what is yours, not to waste your energies on what won't gain you anything or increase your possessions, and not to attempt anything which you don't think you have more than a chance of achieving.

Taureans do have taste; not only taste for food, which they love, but artistic taste, which they develop as a means of distinguishing things of value which they would then like to acquire and gain pleasure from owning. Unlike the Capricorn way of doing things, which values quality because it is valued by others, Taureans enjoy their possessions for themselves. The drawback to the Taurean approach is the lack of enterprise, and the unwillingness to try things just for the fun of it.

Taurean Ascendant people have throat and glandular problems, and all problems associated with being overweight. They can also have back and kidney problems caused as a result of an unwillingness to let things go in their external life. A lighter touch is needed in the approach to problems of possession; shedding unwanted or outworn things in a desirable process.

Gemini Ascendant
If you have a Gemini Ascendant you were born around breakfast time. You should have expressive hands and a wide range of gestures which you use as you speak (ask your friends!) and you are perhaps a little taller than average, or than other members of your family. Gemini Ascendant people also have dark hair, if there is any possibility of it in their parents' colouring, and quick, penetrating eyes which flash with amusement and mischief; Gemini Ascendant women have very fine eyes indeed.

The Gemini approach to things, which you find yourself

using, is one in which the idea of a thing is seen as being the most useful, and in which no time must be lost in telling it to other people so that they can contribute their own ideas and responses to the discussion. The performance of the deed is of no real importance in the Gemini view; somebody else can do that. Ideas and their development are what you like to spend time on, and finding more people to talk to, whose ideas can be matched to your own, seems to you to offer the most satisfaction.

There are two snags to the Gemini approach. The first is that there is a surface quality to it all, in which the rough outline suffices, but no time is spent in development or long-term experience. It may seem insignificant, but there is some value in seeing a project through to the end. The second snag is similar, but is concerned with time. The Gemini approach is immediate, in that it is concerned with the present or the near future. It is difficult for a Gemini Ascendant person to see farther than a few months into the future, if that; it is even more difficult for him to extend his view sideways in time to see the impact of his actions on a wider scene. Both of these things he will dismiss as unimportant.

Gemini Ascendant people suffer from chest and lung maladies, especially when they cannot communicate what they want to or need to, or when they cannot circulate socially in the way that they would like. They also have problems eliminating wastes from their bodies, through not realizing the importance of ending things as well as beginning them. In both cases, thinking and planning on a broader scale than usual, and examination of the past to help make better use of the future, is beneficial.

Cancer Ascendant

You were born mid-morning if you have a Cancer Ascendant and a Taurus Sun. The Cancerian frame, through which you project your Taurean energies, may mean that you appear a little round and not so muscular as other Taureans. Your energies are in no way diminished; in fact, you are likely to be even more determined, and be described in newspaper clichés like 'small and soft to look at, but with a will of steel'. Your face could be almost cherubic, and you could have small features in a pale complexion with grey eyes and brown hair. The key to the Cancer frame is that it is paler than usual, less well defined, and has no strong colouring. Strong noses and red hair do not come from a Cancerian Ascendant.

The Cancerian approach to things is highly personal. All general criticisms are taken personally, and all problems in any procedure for which they have responsibility is seen as a personal failing. As a Taurean with a Cancerian way of working, you will be concerned to use your energies for the safe and secure establishment of things from the foundations up, so that you know that whatever you have been involved in has been done properly, and is unlikely to let you down in any way; you are concerned for your own safety and reputation. The other side of this approach is that you can be a little too concerned to make sure everything is done personally, and be unwilling to entrust things to other people. Not only does this overwork you, it seems obsessive and uncooperative to others.

The Cancer Ascendant person has health problems with the maintenance of the flow of fluids in his body, and a tendency to stomach ulcers caused by worry. Cancer Ascendant women should pay special attention to their breasts, since the affinity between the sign, the Moon as ruler of all things feminine, and that particular body system means that major imbalances in the life are likely to show there first. There could also be some problems with the liver and the circulation of the legs; the answer is to think that, metaphorically, you do not have to support everybody you know: they can use their own legs to stand on, and you do not have to feed them either.

Leo Ascendant

You were born around noon if you have Leo as an Ascendant sign. This will make for great success in your chosen career, whatever it is. Whatever the job title, Taureans do things the way that seems best to them, whether or not they are recognized for it, but being born around the middle of the day guarantees public prominence whether you want it or not. Leo, as the determinant of the physical characteristics, makes itself known by the lion of the sign—you can always spot the deep chest, proud and slightly pompous way of walking, and, more often than not, the hair arranged in some sort of a mane, either full or taken back off the face, and golden if possible. Leo Ascendant people have strong voices and a definite presence to them. Taurus Sun and Leo Ascendant will bring to the fore any hereditary tendency to golden or red colouring, so a flushed complexion, or coppery hair, or even freckles, may be in evidence, as will a heavy build in the upper half of the body.

The Leonine way of doing things is to put yourself in the centre and work from the centre outwards, making sure that everybody knows where the commands are coming from. It is quite a tiring way of working; you need to put a lot of energy into it, because you are acting as the driving force for everybody else. Preferred situations for this technique are those where you already know, more or less, what's going to happen; this way you are unlikely to be thrown off balance by unexpected develop-ments. The grand gesture belongs to the Leo method; it works best if all processes are converted into theatrical scenes, with roles acted rather than lived. Over-reaction, over-dramatization, and over-indulgence are common, but the approach is in essence kind-hearted and well-meant. Children enjoy being with Leo Ascendant people, and they enjoy having children around them. The flaws in the approach are only that little gets done in difficult circumstances where applause and appreciation are scarce commodities, and that little is attempted that is really new and innovatory.

The health problems of the Leo Ascendant person come from the heart, and also from the joints, which suffer from mobility problems. These both come from a lifetime of being at the centre of things and working for everybody's good, and from being too stiff and unwilling to try any change in position. The remedy, of course, is to be more flexible, and to allow your friends to repay the favours they owe you.

Virgo Ascendant

An early afternoon birth puts Virgo on the Ascendant. Physically, this should make you slim and rather long, especially in the body; even if you have broad shoulders you will still have a long waist. There is a neatness to the features, but nothing notable; hair is brown, but again nothing notable. The nose and chin are often well-defined, and the forehead is often both tall and broad; the voice can be a little shrill and lacks penetration.

The Virgoan Ascendant person does not have an approach to life; he has a *system*. He analyses everything and pays a lot of attention to the way in which he works. It is important to the person with Virgo rising not only to be effective, but to be efficient; you can always interest them in a new or better technique. They watch themselves work, as if from a distance, all the while wondering if they can do it better. They never mind repetition; in fact they quite enjoy it, because as they get more proficient they feel better about things. A Taurean with a Virgo Ascendant will want to know how anything and everything works; you will not be able to take anything for granted, and will have to devote all your attention to things until you have mastered their intricacies for yourself. There is a willingness to help others, to be of service through being able to offer a superior technique, inherent in the Virgo way of doing things, which prevents Virgo rising people from being seen as cold and unfriendly. They appreciate their help being appreciated. The problems in the Virgo attitude are a tendency to go into things in more detail than is necessary, and to be too much concerned with the 'proper' way to do things.

People with a Virgo Ascendant are susceptible to intestinal problems and circulatory problems, and may be prone to poor sight. All of these are ways in which the body registers the stresses of being too concerned with digesting the minutiae of things which are meant to be passed through anyway, and by not getting enough social contact. The remedy is to lift your head from your workbench sometimes, admit that the act is sometimes more important than the manner of its performance, and not to take things too seriously.

Libra Ascendant

You were born in the middle of the afternoon if you have Libra rising; it will soften the impact of your Taurean bullishness on others. You should be tallish, and graceful, as all Libra Ascendant people tend to be, have a clear complexion, and often blue eyes, set in an oval face with finely-formed features.

The Libra Ascendant person has to go through life at a fairly relaxed pace. The sign that controls his body won't let him feel rushed or anxious; if that sort of thing looks likely, then he will slow down a little until the panic's over. There is a need to see yourself reflected in the eyes of others, and so you will form a large circle of friends. You define your own opinion of yourself through their responses to you, rather than being sure what you want, and not caring what they think.

The drawback to the Libran approach is that unless you have approval from others, you are unlikely to do anything on your own initiative, or at least you find it hard to decide on a course of action. You always want to do things in the way which will cause the least bother to anyone, and to produce an acceptable overall result; sometimes this isn't definite enough, and you need to know what you do want as well as what you don't.

The Libran Ascendant makes the body susceptible to all ailments of the kidneys and of the skin; there may also be trouble in the feet. The kidney ailments are from trying to take all the problems out of life as you go along. Sometimes it's better simply to attack a few of the obstacles and knock them flat in pure rage.

Scorpio Ascendant

You were probably born towards sunset if you have Scorpio for your Ascendant sign. It should give you a dark and powerful look, with a solid build, though not necessarily over-muscled, Scorpio Ascendant people tend to have a very penetrating and level way of looking at others, which is often disconcerting. Any possible darkness in the colouring is usually displayed, with dark complexions and dark hair, often thick and curly, never fine.

The Scorpio Ascendant person usually does things in a controlled manner. He is not given to explosive releases of energy unless they are absolutely necessary; even then, not often. He knows, or feels (a better word, since the Scorpionic mind makes decisions as a result of knowledge gained by feeling rather than thinking), that he has plenty of energy to spare, but uses it in small and effective doses, each one suited to the requirements of the task at hand. It does not seem useful to him to put in more effort than is strictly necessary for any one activity; that extra energy could be used somewhere else. The idea that overdoing things for their own sake is sometimes fun because of the sheer exhilaration of the release of energy does not strike a responsive chord in the Scorpio body, nor even much understanding. There is, however, understanding and perception of a situation which exists at more than one level. If anything is complicated, involving many activities and many people, with much interaction and many side issues which must be considered, then the Scorpio Ascendant person sees it all and understands all of it, in its minutest detail. They feel, and understand, the responses from all of their surroundings at once, but do not necessarily feel involved with them unless they choose to make a move. When they do move, they will have the intention of transforming things, making them different to conform to their ideas of how things need to be arranged.

Scorpio Ascendant people are unable simply to possess and look after anything; they must change it and direct it their way, and this can be a disadvantage.

Scorpio illnesses are usually to do with the genital and excretory systems; problems here relate to a lifestyle in which things are thrown away when used, or sometimes rejected when there is still use in them. It may be that there is too much stress on being the founder of the new, and on organizing others; this will bring head pains, and illnesses of that order. The solution is to take on the existing situation as it is, and look after it without changing any of it.

Sagittarius Ascendant

It would have been just after sunset when you were born for you
to have a Sagittarius Ascendant. If you have, you should be taller
than average, with a sort of sporty, leggy look to you; you should
have a long face with pronounced temples (you may be balding
there if you are male), a well-coloured complexion, clear eyes, and
brown hair. A Grecian nose is sometimes a feature of this
physique.

The Sagittarian Ascendant gives a way of working that is based
on mobility and change. This particular frame can't keep still
and is much more comfortable walking than standing, more
comfortable lounging or leaning than sitting formally. You tend
to be in a bit of a hurry; travelling takes up a lot of your time,
because you enjoy it so. It is probably true to say that you enjoy
the process of driving more than whatever it is that you have to
do when you get there. You probably think a lot of your car, and
you are likely to have one which is more than just a machine for
transport—you see it as an extension, a representation even, of
yourself. People will notice how outgoing and friendly you seem
to be, but they will need to know you for some time before they
realize that you enjoy meeting people more than almost anything
else, and you dislike being with the same companions all the
time. There is a constant restlessness in you; you will feel that
being static is somehow unnatural, and it worries you. You are an
optimist, but can also be an opportunist, in that you see no
reason to stay doing one thing for a moment longer than it
interests you. The inability to stay and develop a situation or give
long-term commitment to anything is the biggest failing of this
sign's influence.

A person with Sagittarius rising can expect to have problems
with his hips and thighs, and possibly in his arterial system; this
is to do with trying to leap too far at once, in all senses. You may
also have liver and digestive problems, again caused by haste on
a long-term scale. The remedy is to shorten your horizons and
concentrate on things nearer home.

Capricorn Ascendant

It would have been well into the evening when you were born for you to have a Capricorn Ascendant. This sign often gives a small frame, quite compact and built to last a long time, the sort that doesn't need a lot of feeding and isn't big enough or heavy enough to break when it falls over. The face can be narrow and the features small; often the mouth points downwards at the corners, and this doesn't change even when the person smiles or laughs.

The Capricorn sees life as an ordered, dutiful struggle. There is a great deal of emphasis placed on projecting and maintaining appearances, both in the professional and the personal life; the idea of 'good reputation' is one which everybody with Capricorn rising, whatever their sun sign, recognizes at once. There is a sense of duty and commitment which the Sagittarian Ascendant simply cannot understand; here the feeling is that there are things which need doing, so you just have to set to and get them done. Capricorn Ascendant people see far forwards in time, anticipating their responsibilities for years to come, even if their Sun sign does not normally function this way; in such cases they apply themselves to one problem at a time, but can envisage a succession of such problems, one after another, going on for years.

The disadvantages of this outlook are to do with its static nature. There is often a sense of caution that borders on the paranoid, and while this is often well disguised in affluent middle-class middle age, it seems a little odd in the young. This tends to make for a critical assessment of all aspects of a new venture before embarking on it, and as a result a lot of the original impetus is lost. This makes the result less than was originally hoped in many cases, and so a cycle of disappointment and unadventurousness sets in, which is difficult to break. The Capricorn Ascendant person is often humourless, and can seem determined to remain so.

These people have trouble in their joints, and break bones from time to time, entirely as a result of being inflexible. On a small scale this can be from landing badly in an accident because the Capricorn Ascendant keeps up appearances to the very end, refusing to believe that an accident could be happening to him: on a large scale, a refusal to move with the times can lead to the collapse of an outmoded set of values when they are swept away by progress, and this breaking up of an old structure can also cripple. They can get lung troubles, too, as a result of not taking enough fresh air, or fresh ideas. The best treatment is to look after their families rather than their reputation, and to think about the difference between stability and stagnation.

Aquarius Ascendant
Having an Aquarius Ascendant means that you were born around midnight. This will make you chattier than you would otherwise have been, with a strong interest in verbal communication. There is a certain clarity, not to say transparency, about the Aquarian physique. It is usually tall, fair, and well shaped, almost never small or dark. There is nothing about the face which is particularly distinctive; no noticeable colouring, shape of nose, brows, or any other feature. It is an average sort of face, cleanly formed and clear.

The person with an Aquarian Ascendant wants to be independent. Not violently so, not the sort of independence that fights its way out of wherever it feels it's been put, just different from everybody else. Aquarius gives your body the ability to do things in ways perhaps not done before; you can discover new techniques and practices for yourself, and don't need to stay in the ways you were taught. There is a willingness to branch out, to try new things; not a Scorpionic wish to make things happen the way you want, but an amused curiosity which would just like to see if things are any better done a different way. There is no need for you to convince the world that your way is best: it only needs to suit you.

Of course, an Aquarian needs to measure his difference against others, and therefore you feel better when you have a few friends around you to bounce ideas off, as well as showing them how you're doing things in a slightly different way. You function best in groups, and feel physically at ease when you're not the only person in the room. You are not necessarily the leader of the group; just a group member. Group leaders put their energy into the group, and you draw strength and support from it, so you are unlikely to be the leader, though paradoxically all groups work better for having you in them.

A handicap arising from an Aquarian Ascendant is that you are unlikely to really feel passionately involved with anything, and this may mean that unless you have support from your friends and colleagues you will be unable to muster the determination necessary to overcome really sizeable obstacles in your chosen career.

You are likely to suffer from diseases of the circulation and in your lower legs and ankles; these may reflect a life where too much time is spent trying to be independent, and not enough support is sought from others. You may also get stomach disorders and colds because you are not generating enough heat: get more involved in things and angrier about them!

Pisces Ascendant
You were born in the early hours of the morning if you have Pisces rising. Like Aries rising, Pisces is only possible as an Ascendant for about fifty minutes, so there aren't many of you around. Pisces Ascendant people are on the small side, with a tendency to be a bit pale and fleshy. They are not very well coordinated and so walk rather clumsily, despite the fact that their feet are often large. They have large, expressive, but rather sleepy-looking eyes.

As a Taurus with Pisces rising, you will be very concerned for your own safety; you will respond to any possible threat with the greatest possible speed, and that response will not be to charge your attacker, as other Taureans sometimes do. You will retire to your own world, secure in your own favourite thoughts and creature comforts, until the danger has gone away. You will be particularly sensitive to emotional states, and the moods of others; you will be able to feel at once if there is any animosity towards you, and will be very careful to ensure your own emotional happiness. There is a lack of mental resilience here which gives an inability to ignore other people's reactions to you; paradoxically, you are fascinated to see what these will be, and enjoy any stimulation your emotions can get—whilst hoping that you are going to like all you hear. As a Piscean you need variety and stimulation, but as a Taurean you need reassurance.

The major problem with a Pisces Ascendant is the inability to be active rather than reactive; to you there are too many possibilities for a single one to be decided upon. True, with a Taurus Sun this tendency is lessened, and once you have decided to act you will at least be consistent in your action, but you will still be reacting to outside influences rather than generating your own movements from within yourself.

A Piscean Ascendant gives problems with the feet and the lymphatic system; this has connections with the way you move in response to external pressures, and how you deal with things which invade your system from outside. You may also suffer from faint-heartedness—literally as well as metaphorically. The remedy is to be more definite and less influenced by opinions other than your own.

6. Three Crosses: Areas of Life that Affect Each Other

If you have already determined your Ascendant sign from page 71, and you have read 'The Meaning of the Zodiac' on page 11, you can apply that knowledge to every area of your life with revealing results. Instead of just looking at yourself, you can see how things like your career and your finances work from the unique point of view of your birth moment.

You will remember how the Ascendant defined which way up the sky was. Once you have it the right way up, then you can divide it into sectors for different areas of life, and see which zodiac signs occupy them. After that, you can interpret each sector of sky in the light of what you know about the zodiac sign which fell in it at the time that you were born.

Below there is a circular diagram of the sky, with the horizon splitting it across the middle. This is the way real horoscopes are usually drawn. In the outer circle, in the space indicated, write the name of your Ascendant sign, not your Sun sign (unless they are the same, of course. If you don't know your time of birth, and so can't work out an Ascendant, use your Sun sign). Make it overlap sectors 12 and 1, so that the degree of your Ascendant within that sign is on the eastern horizon. Now fill in the rest of the zodiac around the circle in sequence, one across each sector boundary. If you've forgotten the sequence, look at the diagram on page 16. When you've done that, draw a symbol for the Sun (☉—a circle with a point at its centre) in one of the sectors which has your Sun sign at its edge. Think about how far through the sign your Sun is; make sure that you have put it in the right sector. Whichever sector this is will be very important to you;

having the Sun there gives a bias to the whole chart, like the weight on one side of a locomotive wheel. You will feel that the activities of that sector (or house, as they are usually called) are most in keeping with your character, and you feel comfortable doing that sort of thing.

Make sure you have got your sums right. As a Taurean born in the middle of the afternoon, you might well have Virgo rising, and the Sun in the eighth house, for example.

Now is the time to examine the twelve numbered sections of your own sky, and see what there is to be found.

Angular Houses: 1, 4, 7, 10

These are the houses closest to the horizon and the vertical, reading round in zodiacal sequence. The first house is concerned with you yourself as a physical entity, your appearance, and your health. Most of this has been dealt with in the section on

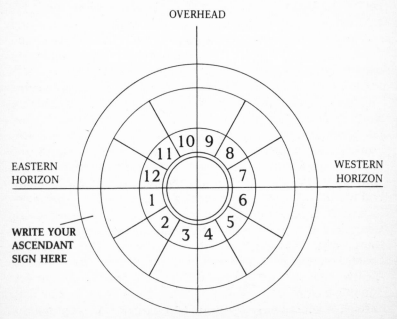

Ascendants. If you have the Sun here, it simply doubles the impact of your Sun sign energies.

Opposite to you is the seventh house, which concerns itself with everybody who is not you. Partners in a business sense, husbands, wives, enemies you are actually aware of (and who therefore stand opposed to you in plain sight) and any other unclassified strangers all belong in the seventh house. You see their motivation as being of the opposite sign to your Ascendant sign, as being something you are not. If you have Capricorn rising, you see them as behaving, and needing to be treated, which is perhaps more accurate, in a Cancerian manner. This is how you approach seventh-house things. Use the keywords from 'The Meaning of the Zodiac' (p. 17) to remind yourself what this is. If you have the Sun in the seventh house you are your own best partner: you may marry late in life, or not at all. Perhaps your marriage will be unsuccessful. It is not a failure; it is simply that you are to a very great extent self-supporting, and have neither the ability nor the need to share yourself completely with another.

The whole business of the first and the seventh is to do with 'me and not-me'. For the personal energies of this relationship to be shown in tangible form, it is necessary to look at the pair of houses whose axis most squarely crosses the first/seventh axis. This is the fourth/tenth. The tenth is your received status in the world, and is the actual answer to the question 'What do you take me for?' No matter what you do, the world will find it best to see you as doing the sort of thing shown by the sign at the start of the tenth house. Eventually, you will start to pursue that kind of activity anyway, because in doing so you get more appreciation and reward from the rest of society.

Your efforts in dealing with others, which is a first/seventh thing, have their result in the tenth, and their origins in the fourth. Expect to find clues there to your family, your home, the beliefs you hold most dear, and the eventual conclusion to your life (not your death, which is a different matter). If you have the Sun in the tenth, you will achieve some measure of prominence or fame; if your Sun is in the fourth, you will do well in property, and your family will be of greater importance to you than is usual.

There is, of course, some give and take between the paired houses. Giving more time to yourself in the first house means that you are denying attention to the seventh, your partner; the reverse also applies. Giving a lot of attention to your career, in the tenth house, stops you from spending quite so much time as you might like with your family or at home. Spending too much time at home means that you are out of the public eye. There is only so much time in a day; what you give to one must be denied to the other.

This cross of four houses defines most people's lives: self, partner, home, and career. An over-emphasis on any of these is to the detriment of the other three, and all the arms of the cross feel and react to any event affecting any single member.

If these four houses have cardinal signs on them in your chart, then you are very much the sort of person who feels that he is in control of his own life, and that it is his duty to shape it into something new, personal, and original. You feel that by making decisive moves with your own circumstances you can actually change the way your life unfolds, and enjoy steering it the way you want it to go.

If these four houses have fixed signs on them in your chart, then you are the sort of person who sees the essential shape of your life as being one of looking after what you were given, continuing in the tradition, and ending up with a profit at the end of it all. Like a farmer, you see yourself as a tenant of the land you inherited, with a responsibility to hand it on in at least as good a condition as it was when you took it over. You are likely to see the main goal in all life's ups and downs as the maintenance of stability and enrichment of what you possess.

If these four houses have mutable signs on them in your chart, then you are much more willing to change yourself to suit circumstances than the other two. Rather than seeing yourself as the captain of your ship, or the trustee of the family firm, you see yourself as free to adapt to challenges as they arise, and if necessary to make fundamental changes in your life, home and career to suit the needs of the moment. You are the sort to welcome change and novelty, and you don't expect to have anything to show for it at the end of the day except experience. There is a strong sense of service in the mutable signs, and if you spend your life working for the welfare of others, then they will have something to show for it while you will not. Not in physical terms, anyway; you will have had your reward by seeing your own energies transformed into their success.

The Succedent Houses: 2, 5, 8, 11

These houses are called succedent because they succeed, or follow on from, the previous four. Where the angular houses define the framework of the life, the succedent ones give substance, and help develop it to its fullest and richest extent, in exactly the same way as fixed signs show the development and maintenance of the elemental energies defined by the cardinal signs.

The second house and the eighth define your resources; how much you have to play with, so to speak. The fifth and eleventh show what you do with it, and how much you achieve. Your immediate environment is the business of the second house. Your tastes in furniture and clothes are here (all part of your immediate environment, if you think about it) as well as your immediate resources, food and cash. Food is a resource because without it you are short of energy, and cash is a resource for obvious reasons. If you have the Sun here you are likely to be fond of spending money, and fond of eating too! You are likely to place value on things that you can buy or possess, and judge your success by your bank balance.

Opposed to it, and therefore dealing with the opposite viewpoint, is the eighth house, where you will find stored money. Savings, bank accounts, mortgages, and all kinds of non-immediate money come under this house. So do major and irreversible changes in your life, because they are the larger environment rather than the immediate one. Surgical operations and death are both in the eighth, because you are not the same person afterwards, and that is an irreversible change. If you have the Sun in the eighth you are likely to be very careful with yourself, and not the sort to expose yourself to any risk; you are also not likely to be short of a few thousand when life gets tight, because eighth house people always have some extra resource tucked away somewhere. You are also likely to benefit from legacies, which are another form of long-term wealth.

To turn all this money into some form of visible wealth you must obviously do something with it, and all forms of self-expression and ambition are found in the fifth and the eleventh houses. The fifth is where you have fun, basically; all that you like to do, all that amuses you, all your hobbies are found there, and a look at the zodiac sign falling in that house in your chart will show you what it is that you like so much. Your children are a fifth-house phenomenon, too; they are an expression of yourself made physical, made from the substance of your body and existence, and given their own. If you have the Sun in the fifth house you are likely to be of a generally happy disposition, confident that life is there to be enjoyed, and sure that something good will turn up.

The eleventh house, in contrast, is not so much what you like doing as what you would like to be doing: it deals with hopes, wishes, and ambitions. It also deals with friends and all social gatherings, because in a similar manner to the first/seventh axis, anybody who is 'not-you' and enjoying themselves must be opposed to you enjoying yourself in the fifth house. If you have the Sun in the eleventh house, you are at your best in a group. You would do well in large organizations, possibly political ones, and will find that you can organize well. You have well-defined ambitions, and know how to realize them, using other people as supporters of your cause.

The oppositions in this cross work just as effectively as the previous set did: cash is either used or stored, and to convert it from one to the other diminishes the first. Similarly, time spent enjoying yourself does nothing for your ambitions and aims, nor does it help you maintain relationships with all the groups of people you know; there again, all work and no play . . .

If you have cardinal signs on these four houses in your chart, then you think that using all the resources available to you at any one time is important. Although what you do isn't necessarily important, or even stable, you want to have something to show for it, and enjoying yourself as you go along is important to you. To you, money is for spending, and how your friends see you is possibly more important to you than how you see yourself.

Fixed signs on these four houses will make you reticent, and careful of how you express yourself. You are possibly too busy with the important things of life as you see them, such as your career and long-term prospects, to give much attention to the way you live. You feel it is important to have things of quality, because you have a long-term view of life, and you feel secure when you have some money in the bank, but you don't enjoy your possessions and friends for your own sake. You have them because you feel that you should, not because they are reason enough in themselves.

Mutable signs on these four houses show a flexible attitude to the use of a resource, possibly because the angular houses show that you already have plenty of it, and it is your duty to use it well. You don't mind spending time and money on projects which to you are necessary, and which will have a measurable end result. You see that you need to spend time and effort to bring projects into a completed reality, and you are willing to do that as long as the final product is yours and worth having. You are likely to change your style of living quite frequently during your life, and there may be ambitions which, when fulfilled, fade from your life completely.

The Cadent Houses: 3, 6, 9, 12

The final four houses are called cadent either because they fall away from the angles (horizon and vertical axes), or because they fall towards them, giving their energy towards the formation of the next phase in their existence. Either way, affairs in these

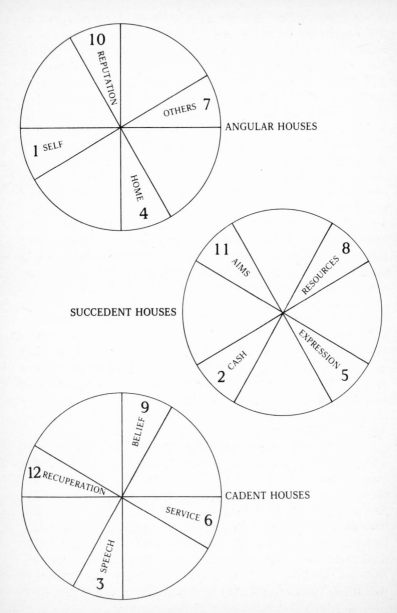

ANGULAR HOUSES

SUCCEDENT HOUSES

CADENT HOUSES

houses are nothing like as firm and active as those in the other two sets of four. It may be useful to think of them as being given to mental rather than physical or material activities.

The third and ninth houses are given to thought and speech, with the ninth specializing in incoming thoughts, such as reading, learning and belief (religions of all kinds are ninth-house things), while the third limits itself to speaking and writing, daily chat, and the sort of conversations you have every day. If you have the Sun in the third house, you will be a chatterbox. Talking is something you could do all day, and you love reading. Anything will do—papers, magazines, novels; as long as it has words in it you will like it. You will have the sort of mind that loves accumulating trivia, but you may find that serious study or hard learning is something that you cannot do.

The third house concerns itself with daily conversation, but the ninth is more withdrawn. Study is easy for a ninth-house person, but since all ideal and theoretical thought belongs here, the down-to-earth street-corner reality of the third house doesn't, and so the higher knowledge of the ninth finds no application in daily life. The third-ninth axis is the difference between practical street experience and the refined learning of a university. To give time to one must mean taking time from the other. If you have the Sun in the ninth, you are likely to have a very sure grasp of the theory of things, and could well be an instigator or director of large projects; but you are unable to actually do the things yourself. Knowledge is yours, but application is not.

How this knowledge gets applied in the production of something new is a matter of technique, and technique is the business of the sixth house. The way things get done, both for yourself and for other people's benefit, is all in the sixth. Everything you do on someone else's behalf is there, too. If you have the Sun in the sixth house, you are careful and considerate by nature, much concerned to make the best use of things and to do things in the best way possible. Pride of work and craftsman-ship are guiding words to you; any kind of sloppiness is upsetting. You look after yourself, too; health is a sixth-house

thing, and the Sun in the sixth sometimes makes you something
of a hypochondriac.

Opposed to the sixth, and therefore opposed to the ideas of
doing things for others, mastering the proper technique, and
looking after your physical health, is the twelfth house. This is
concerned with withdrawing yourself from the world, being on
your own, having time to think. Energy is applied to the job in
hand in the sixth house, and here it is allowed to grow again
without being applied to anything. Recuperation is a good word
to remember. All forms of rest are twelfth-house concepts. If you
have the Sun in the twelfth house you are an essentially private
individual, and there will be times when you need to be on your
own to think about things and recover your strength and
balance. You will keep your opinions to yourself, and share very
little of your emotional troubles with anyone. Yours is most
definitely not a life lived out in the open.

These houses live in the shadow of the houses which follow
them. Each of them is a preparation for the next phase. If your
Sun is in any of these houses, your life is much more one of
giving away than of accumulation. You already have the
experience and the knowledge, and you will be trying to hand it
on before you go, so to speak. Acquisition is something you will
never manage on a permanent basis.

If these houses have Cardinal signs on them in your chart,
then preparation for things to come is important to you, and you
think in straight lines towards a recognized goal. You will have
firm and rather simplistic views and beliefs about matters which
are not usually described in such terms, such as morality and
politics, and you will be used to saying things simply and with
meaning. Deception and half-truths, even mild exaggeration,
confuse you, because you do not think in that sort of way.

If fixed signs occupy these houses in your horoscope, your
thinking is conservative, and your mind, though rich and varied
in its imagination, is not truly original. You like to collect ideas
from elsewhere and tell yourself that they are your own. You rely
on changing circumstances to bring you variety, and your own
beliefs and opinions stay fixed to anchor you in a changing

world; unfortunately, this can mean a refusal to take in new ideas, shown in your behaviour as a rather appealing old-fashionedness.

Having mutable signs on these houses in your horoscope shows a flexible imagination, though often not a very practical one. Speech and ideas flow freely from you, and you are quick to adapt your ideas to suit the occasion, performing complete changes of viewpoint without effort if required. You seem to have grasped the instinctive truth that mental images and words are not real, and can be changed or erased at will; you are far less inhibited in their use than the other two groups, who regard words as something at least as heavy as cement, and nearly as difficult to dissolve. Periods in the public eye and periods of isolation are of equal value to you; you can use them each for their best purpose, and have no dislike of either. This great flexibility of mind does mean, though, that you lack seriousness of approach at times, and have a happy-go-lucky view of the future, and of things spiritual, which may lead to eventual disappointments and regrets.

Houses are important in a horoscope. The twelve sectors of the sky correspond to the twelve signs of the zodiac, the difference being that the zodiac is a product of the Sun's annual revolution, and the houses are a product (via the Ascendant) of the Earth's daily revolution. They bring the symbolism down one level from the sky to the individual, and they answer the questions which arise when people of the same Sun sign have different lives and different preferences. The house in which the Sun falls, and the qualities of the signs in the houses, show each person's approach to those areas of his life, and the one which will be the most important to him.

Part 4

Taurus Trivia

7. Tastes and Preferences

Clothes

Taureans are very fond of their clothes; they like them to reflect
their own idea of themselves, and to show everyone else how
nice they are. Since you like to touch things, you will like to
touch your clothes too, and that means that you will not like
clothes which have a disagreeable feel to them. Synthetics are
not a large part of your wardrobe; natural fabrics are much nicer
to the touch, and because they come from the land rather than
the laboratory you will prefer them. You have a marked
preference for silk—I don't know whether it is because of its
extreme softness to the touch, or because it is expensive, and is
therefore something you can treat yourself to as a declaration of
wealth and security, or whether it is simply that silk tends to be
made into more elegant clothes because of its rarity, and it is the
quality of the cut and colour that attract you. Whatever it is, silk
attracts you, as does any other soft luxury fabric, such as
cashmere.

You don't like your clothes too tight because the build of a
Taurean looks a little, well, trussed up in tight clothes. Because
you move slowly and sometimes a little heavily, you have
learned to let the cut of the clothes do all the work for you, so
that you look well-dressed when standing still. Taureans look
quite majestic when stationary, and you will obviously capitalize

on this. Male Taureans look good in well-made suits with plenty of room in them to give an impression of wealth and comfort, and female Taureans look good in anything which isn't too closely cut and which gives an impression of womanliness without girlishness.

Favourite colours are green and pink—Venus's colours—and there is often a link to the element of Earth in that floral designs seem to be eternally popular with the sign. Taurean men often affect 'farmer's fashion', whereby they wear green and brown a lot, with tweed jackets and comfortable brogues. Such clothes are usually comfortable and soft to the touch, and have a reassuring 'countryside' feeling to them, suggesting a placid and timeless existence of rural contentment which appeals very much to the Taurean psyche. Taurean women have wonderful colour sense, and an unerring eye for the best made dress on the rail, which usually turns out to be the most expensive. This discovery serves to reassure her that her taste is indeed as fine as she knew it to be, and the purchase is made without delay.

Whenever you see someone whose clothes are well-made, well-fitting, not particularly avant-garde or up-to-the-minute, but which do a lot for their wearer without the wearer needing to do much with them, then you are looking at Taurean taste.

Food and Furnishings

Taureans love food. It's as simple as that. They also like the process of eating, and they like the food to be as substantial as they are, so they are not the sort of people to pick daintily at the hors d'oeuvres and then declare that they are full. As cooks, they put a great deal of effort into the preparation of food, and particularly its tasting and testing; their most sensitive sense is that of taste, and they like to do more with that than with any other. They are not particularly innovative cooks; they have a feeling for traditional recipes, and enjoy maintaining that tradition.

A Taurean likes to eat meat, and to eat plenty of it. A good roast is the heart of a satisfying meal for a Taurean, and he will take as much of it as he thinks he can manage, then eat it in a steady manner at his own pace until finished, enjoying every mouthful. It is difficult for other people to understand the satisfaction that a Taurean gets out of food. Other people eat to keep going, or to be sociable, or for something to do: but food is a spiritual thing for a Taurean. It nourishes every part of him, both body and soul, and must not be rushed or ignored. Show this book to your friends so that they will believe it at last.

Apart from meat, Taureans eat everything else in season, although they are not great fish eaters. They like all luxury foods—caviare, asparagus—and all rich foods, especially those which have been enriched by that archetypical Taurean product, cream. They also like heavy desserts; cream and chocolate: anything will be fine as long as there is a lot of it. Their sweet tooth is legendary.

A Taurean house is a very comfortable place. It is always very well furnished, but the prime purpose of all the money that has gone into it is to make it very comfortable, rather than be something with which to impress one's friends. Of course, if you do find it impressive, and point this out to your Taurean host, it will be much appreciated, because the secondary aim *is* to impress—but the primary aim is comfort.

There will be soft furnishings throughout; velvet curtains, deep carpets, and cushions on all the chairs. Colours will be green and pink again, and floral designs, especially chintz, will be much in evidence. Even if there are no floral designs, there will be flowers around, usually in pleasing arrangements. Taureans like flowers, and they like exercising their sense of colour and balance, so they buy (or grow) large amounts of flowers and spend happy hours arranging them. There is usually other evidence of artistic thought, too; pictures on the walls rather than objects, and usually something musical, such as a piano, or at the least a record player.

Hobbies

For hobbies and leisure activity, the Taurean has two areas of talent which he can easily develop. The first is his sense of colour and sound; almost any musical activity from singing to conducting will give him satisfaction, and almost any activity in the Fine Arts will do the same. Painting, sculpting (so strongly material and permanent! Ideal for the Taurean mind), or any handicraft will appeal, and can be done well. Some Taureans, in fact quite a lot of them, have become interior designers and decorators because these careers combine a sense of colour with a physical activity where you work at your own pace. Many Taurean women find themselves in the beauty or fashion business where their feel for colour and fabric finds expression. The second area is the Taurean's affinity with the earth itself. Gardening, long country walks, and any rural pursuit are all very relaxing to Taureans. Again, many have become farmers because the career can offer so much of what they really like and need. Taureans must not feel in any way ashamed of their liking for quiet and the country; the closer they are to the land, the better they are in every way.

8. Taurean Luck

Being lucky isn't a matter of pure luck. It can be engineered.
What happens when you are lucky is that a number of
correspondences are made between circumstances, people, and
even material items, which eventually enable planetary energies
to flow quickly and effectively to act with full force in a
particular way. If you are part of that chain, or your intentions lie
in the same direction as the planetary flow, then you say that
things are going your way, or that you are lucky. All you have to
do to maximize this tendency is to make sure you are aligned to
the flow of energies from the planets whenever you want things
to work your way.

It is regular astrological practice to try to reinforce your own
position in these things, by attracting energies which are already
strongly represented in you. For a Taurean, this means Venus, of
course, and therefore any 'lucky' number, colour, or whatever
for a Taurean is simply going to be one that corresponds
symbolically with the attributes of Venus.

Venus' colour is green; therefore a Taurus person's lucky
colour is green—because by wearing it or aligning himself to it
for example by betting on a horse whose jockey's silks are green,
or supporting a football team whose colours include green—he
aligns himself to the energies of Venus, and thereby recharges
the Venusian energies that are already in him.

A Taurus' preferred gemstone is an emerald, because of its

colour and the reasons given above. Gemstones are seen as being able to concentrate or focus magical energies and the colour of the stone shows its correspondence with the energies of a particular planet. Other gemstones are sometimes quoted for Taurus, such as the moonstone or topaz, but in all cases the colour is the key.

Because Taurus is the second sign, your lucky number is 2; all combinations of numbers which add up to 2 by reduction work the same way, so you have a range to choose from. Reducing a number is done by adding its digits until you can go no further. As an example, take 695, $6 + 9 + 5 = 20$, and then $2 + 0 = 2$. There you are—695 is a lucky number for you, so to buy a car with those digits in its registration plate would make it a car which, while you had it, you were very fond of, and which served you well.

Venus has its own number, which is 7. The same rules apply as they did with 2. Venus also has its own day, Friday (vendredi in French means Venus' day), and Taurus has both a time with which it is associated (the hour before sunrise) and a direction (the South). If you have something important to do, and you manage to put it into action at dawn on Friday 7 February (month number 2, remember), then you will have made sure that you will get the result best suited to you, by aligning yourself to your own planet and helping its energies flow through you and your activity unimpeded.

Venus also has a metal associated with it, and in the Middle Ages people wore jewellery made of their planetary metals for luck, or self-alignment and emphasis, whichever way you want to describe it. In the case of Taurus and Venus, that metal is copper, which is a pity in some ways, because personal ornaments made of copper have never been as popular as silver and gold. Perhaps this is why Taureans get such great pleasure from their clothes and food, which are, after all, personal tokens which come from their element, the earth.

There are plants and herbs for each planet, and foods too. Among the edible plants are apples, figs, peaches, walnuts, and elder flowers.

There is almost no end to the list of correspondences between the planets and everyday items, and many more can be made if you have a good imagination. They are lucky for Taureans if you know what makes them so, and if you believe them to be so; the essence of the process lies in linking yourself and the object of your intent with some identifiable token of your own planet, such as its colour or number, and strengthening yourself thereby. The stronger you are, then the more frequently you will be able to achieve the result you want—and that's all that luck is, isn't it?

A Final Word

By the time you reach here, you will have learnt a great deal more about yourself. At least, I hope you have.

You will probably have noticed that I appear to have contradicted myself in some parts of the book, and repeated myself in others, and there are reasons for this. It is quite likely that I have said that your Sun position makes you one way, while your Ascendant makes you the opposite. There is nothing strange about this; nobody is consistent, the same the whole way through—everybody has contradictory sides to their character, and knowing some more about your Sun sign and your Ascendant will help you to label and define those contradictory elements. It won't do anything about dealing with them, though—that's your job, and always has been. The only person who can live your horoscope is you. Astrology won't make your problems disappear, and it never has been able to; it simply defines the problems more clearly, and enables you to look for answers.

Where I have repeated myself it is either to make the point for the benefit of the person who is only going to read that section of the book, or because you have a double helping of the energy of your sign, as in the instance of the Sun and Ascendant in the same sign.

I hope you found the relationships section useful; you may well find that the Sun-to-Ascendant comparison is just as useful in showing you how you fit in with your partner as the usual Sun-to-Sun practice.

Where do you go from here? If you want to learn more about astrology, and see how all of the planets fit into the picture of the sky as it was at your birth, then you must either consult an astrologer or learn how to do it for yourself. There is quite a lot of astrology around these days; evening classes are not too hard to find and there are groups of enthusiasts up and down the country. There are also plenty of books which will show you how to draw up and interpret your own horoscope.

One thing about doing it yourself, which is an annoyance unless you are aware of it in advance: to calculate your horoscope properly you will need to know where the planets were in the sky when you were born, and you usually have to buy this data separately in a book called an ephemeris. The reason that astrology books don't have this data in them is that to include enough for everybody who is likely to buy the book would make the book as big as a phone directory, and look like a giant book of log tables, which is a bit off-putting. You can buy ephemerides (the plural) for any single year, such as the one of your birth. You can also buy omnibus versions for the whole century.

So, you will need two books, not one: an ephemeris, and a book to help you draw up and interpret your horoscope. It's much less annoying when you *know* you're going to need two books.

After that, there are lots of books on the more advanced techniques in the Astrology Handbook series, also from the Aquarian Press. Good though the books are, there is no substitute for being taught by an astrologer, and no substitute at all for practice. What we are trying to do here is provide a vocabulary of symbols taken from the sky so that you and your imagination can make sense of the world you live in; the essential element is your imagination, and you provide that.

Astrology works perfectly well at Sun sign level, and it works perfectly well at deeper levels as well; you can do it with what you want. I hope that, whatever you do with it, it is both instructive and satisfying to you—and fun, too.

SUNS AND LOVERS

The Astrology of Sexual Relationships

Penny Thornton. It doesn't seem to matter how experienced – or inexperienced – you are, when it comes to love and romance there just *isn't* a fool proof formula. . . but this book does its best to provide one! THE definitive astrological guide to sexual relationships, this book is based upon the accumulated wisdom, and observations of centuries of dedicated astrologers. Reveals:

- In-depth analysis of astrological types
- Male and female profiles for each star sign
- Zodiacal attitudes to intimate relationships
- Most compatible – and incompatible – partners

Each general star sign analysis is concluded with amazingly frank reflections, often based upon personal interviews, with many famous personalities including: Bob Champion; Suzi Quatro; Colin Wilson; Jeremy Irons; HRH The Princess Anne; HRH The Duke of York; Martin Shaw; Barbara Cartland; Twiggy and many more. Written in an easy-to-read style, and packed with illuminating and fascinating tit-bits, this book is compulsive reading for anyone likely to have *any sort* of encounter with the opposite sex!

HOW TO ASTRO-ANALYSE YOURSELF AND OTHERS.

Mary Coleman. Easy to follow, step-by-step instructions on the art of astro-analysis a blend of traditional astrology and modern psychology that provides practical solutions to the conundrums of life, love and sex.

- Discover why you do the things you do.
- Plan your life instead of just 'letting it happen'.
- Make the most of yourself and your relationships.

Master the technique of astro-anaysis and discover a more confident 'you' emerging, and the path to a happier, more satisying future opening out before you. The day you read this book could be the first day of the rest of your life.

THE ASTROLOGY WORKBOOK

This book is YOUR introduction to FUN, FORTUNE and FASCINATION

Cordelia Mansall, in clear and easy-to-understand language, de-mystifies the ancient science of astrology and shows how YOU can profit from this exact, and increasingly respected, wisdom.

Discover

- When to expect your 'vitality surges'
- The crisis ages of your life
- Your hidden talents
- The latent potentialities of your children

The whole of our lives are shaped by cosmic forces. Astrology is the study of these forces and their effects upon our lives *both now and in the future*. The author shows how it can be used to bring a deeper understanding to the problems encountered in personal relationships, indicate the most favourable times for major life-style changes and present an important balance between science and spirituality. *Discover your place in the overall scheme of the universe with* THE ASTROLOGY WORKBOOK by **Cordelia Mansall D. F. Astrol. S.**